PRAISE FOR

Fatal Attractions

Jack Hayford has been such a blessing to so many Christians over the
years, and they will all be helped by this sensitive
book on how to overcome the sexual sins that are destroying
marriages and ministries all over the world.

DR. NEIL T. ANDERSON

AUTHOR, *VICTORY OVER THE DARKNESS* AND *FINDING FREEDOM
IN A SEX-OBSESSED WORLD*

I can think of no one more qualified to write a biblical treatise
on this critical subject than Jack Hayford. *Fatal Attractions* is a
masterpiece that builds biblical conviction into the reader and brings
hope and forgiveness for those who are struggling, as well as
encouragement to all to pursue sexual purity.

FRANK DAMAZIO

AUTHOR, *THE MAKING OF A VISION* AND *FOUNDATIONAL TRUTH*
SENIOR PASTOR, CITY BIBLE CHURCH
PORTLAND, OREGON

In *Fatal Attractions*, Jack Hayford presents the plain truth
about sexual temptation and sin. Straightforward yet sensitive,
this book uncovers sexual deception and tenderly reveals the
overarching remedy of redemptive love. With candor and grace, Jack
shares God's desire to restore men and women to the wholeness only
God can provide. *Fatal Attractions* is not only for those who have been
hurt by sexual sin but for parents and Christian leaders as well.

MARILYN HICKEY

AUTHOR, *BREAKING GENE*
PASTOR AND SF
FOUNDER AND PRESIDENT, MARI

D1111914

With more than 40 years of experience speaking to audiences of all ages, Jack Hayford is exceptionally qualified to write about the blessings of sex and the destructiveness of its misuse. To a constantly changing culture, Jack presents rock-solid principles based on the eternal truth of the Bible. *Fatal Attractions* is a must-read for all who are ready to be presented with no-nonsense yet compassionate truth about sex.

JOSH D. MCDOWELL
AUTHOR, *BEYOND BELIEF TO CONVICTIONS* AND *MORE THAN A CARPENTER*
INTERNATIONAL SPEAKER

Jack Hayford, always clear and candid, writes the truth we *all* need to hear about how our senses are being continually bombarded with temptation to cross the line of what is acceptable in the eyes of God in our thought life as well as in our actions. God has a better way, and Jack shows us how to find it. Never has there been a time in our culture when this book has been more needed.

STORMIE OMARTIAN
AUTHOR, *THE POWER OF A PRAYING WIFE*

Jack Hayford has done it again by giving a solid biblical analysis of a perplexing present-day struggle. *Fatal Attractions* is a crucial book for any pastor or counselor who cares for hurting souls. Chapter 4 is especially profound and penetrating, helping us understand that our sexual struggles are not ultimately about sex. These issues lie much deeper in the soul. *Fatal Attractions* is a book you must read.

TED ROBERTS
AUTHOR, *PURE DESIRE*
SENIOR PASTOR, EAST HILL FOURSQUARE CHURCH
GRESHAM, OREGON

Pastor Jack Hayford always hits the target dead center when it comes to critically important issues. He has done it again with *Fatal Attractions*. Jack reveals why sexual extremes lead to such depths of bondage and how we can find freedom. Improper sexual messages saturate today's culture, and unfortunately, biblical truths are being ignored. The Church has much to learn about how to effectively deal with this struggle. I am convinced that *Fatal Attractions* will be a welcome resource for pastors and those who are seeking wholeness.

JAMES ROBISON
FOUNDER AND PRESIDENT, LIFE OUTREACH INTERNATIONAL

When I watch football, I'm concerned that my children will see a commercial or a halftime show that will catapult them out of sexual innocence. Some are crying out for the government to step in and regulate such things. Jack Hayford is calling Christians to step in and prayerfully consider how sex sins write consequences in stone like few other sins can. *Fatal Attractions* is a book that will lead us to bring our sexual lives fully under the lordship of Jesus Christ.

GREG TAYLOR
AUTHOR, *HIGH PLACES* AND *DOWN IN THE RIVER TO PRAY*
MANAGING EDITOR, *NEW WINESKINS* MAGAZINE

Fatal

ATTRACTIONS

Why Sex Sins Are
Worse Than Others

JACK HAYFORD

Regal

From Gospel Light
Ventura, California, U.S.A.

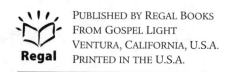

PUBLISHED BY REGAL BOOKS
FROM GOSPEL LIGHT
VENTURA, CALIFORNIA, U.S.A.
PRINTED IN THE U.S.A.

Regal Books is a ministry of Gospel Light, a Christian publisher dedicated to serving the local church. We believe God's vision for Gospel Light is to provide church leaders with biblical, user-friendly materials that will help them evangelize, disciple and minister to children, youth and families.

It is our prayer that this Regal book will help you discover biblical truth for your own life and help you meet the needs of others. May God richly bless you.

For a free catalog of resources from Regal Books/Gospel Light, please call your Christian supplier or contact us at 1-800-4-GOSPEL *or* www.regalbooks.com.

Cover design by David Griffing
Internal design by Stephen Hahn
Edited by Selimah Nemoy

Library of Congress Cataloging-in-Publication Data

Hayford, Jack W.
 Fatal attractions / Jack W. Hayford.
    p. cm.
 Includes bibliographical references.
 ISBN 0-8307-2968-2
 1. Sex—Religious aspects—Christianity. I. Title.
 BT708.H39 2004
 241'.66—dc22   2004006219

2   3   4   5   6   7   8   9   10   11   12   13   14   15   /   10   09   08   07   06   05   04

Rights for publishing this book in other languages are contracted by Gospel Light Worldwide, the international nonprofit ministry of Gospel Light. Gospel Light Worldwide also provides publishing and technical assistance to international publishers dedicated to producing Sunday School and Vacation Bible School curricula and books in the languages of the world. For additional information, visit www.gospellightworldwide.org; write to Gospel Light Worldwide, P.O. Box 3875, Ventura, CA 93006; or send an e-mail to info@gospellightworldwide.org.

CONTENTS

PREFACE

Neither do I condemn you; go and sin no more.

JOHN 8:11

She stood there alone in the chilly gray dawn, trembling in fear, her heart pounding hard enough that she feared it would burst from her chest. She had not been allowed any time to get more than half-dressed before she was brutally dragged from her house and into the town square. Humiliated, frightened and cold, she wrapped her arms around her body in a posture of feeble defense against the rage and torment of her accusers.

"She should die!" yelled the town's most influential religious leader. "Stone the whore!"

"Execute her! The law demands it," echoed the mob behind him, poised with stones already in hand to enforce the death sentence.

Her mind reeled; her soul was filled with shame and terror. The man who had shared her bed had shown up at her door a few hours earlier. She'd seen him once or twice in the village, but she didn't know his name. He had asked if he could come in. The light from an oil lamp had flickered against the walls inside her house as she had studied his face and weighed his proposition. She was no model of purity, but neither was she without feelings. She had been lonely. It had been so long since anyone had looked so deeply into her eyes.

Now all eyes and every heart turned on her in hatred. Except for the eyes of one. Some had called Him a prophet; she had even heard that there were those who believed He might be the Messiah.

"Who among you is without sin?" He demanded. "Let him cast the first stone." Then He stooped down and wrote something in the sand that she could not read. Suddenly, the hearts and minds of the woman's accusers were seared, for not one of them could claim to be without sin. One by one, each laid down his rock and backed away.

John's Gospel account (see John 8:2-11) relates how the Savior stood between the woman guilty of sexual sin and those who would condemn her. He's still willing to do the same today—to stand up for anyone who has sinned in *any* way and become his or her defender. The issue, however, is this: His "standing up" is neither a casual condoning of sin nor a harsh condemning of it; but He *does* confront it. As with the woman trapped by her own sin in an adulterous relationship, Jesus is ready to bring peace and freedom to anyone today who comes with the same openness to His dual word of forgiveness balanced with an assignment to receive His power to "go and sin no more" (John 8:11).

All of us who have received new life in Jesus Christ are grateful for the Savior who stands between us and the death penalty for our sins, sexual or otherwise. So if you have picked up this book looking for answers to help a friend, or if you are reading it in a quest to find answers for yourself, please know that the same Spirit Jesus manifested motivates me in sharing with you. Like the woman in this story, you may have tried to fill the empty, broken places of your life with the corruption this world deceives people into thinking will bring them happiness. And like this woman, you may have found that it brings a death penalty—the stoning of your self-esteem; the trashing of your self-respect; the penalty of a sexually transmitted disease that renders you infertile; an unwanted pregnancy that condemns to death an innocent, unborn soul; the death sentence of AIDS.

More than four decades of being a pastor have convinced me that sex sins are worse than other sins. That does not mean they are harder for God to forgive. And it certainly doesn't mean that I reject people or hold them at a distance because of sexual failure. I don't hold people at a distance by reason of *any* failure. Nor does God. Indeed, the Scriptures declare that God so loved the world—even in its rebellion against Him—that He provided a

Savior in the person of His own Son, Jesus, so that our lives might be redeemed rather than condemned (see John 3:16).

Sex sins are not harder for God to forgive, but they are more *damaging* at a personal and social dimension than other sins. Sexual sin assaults the fountainhead of every great thing that God intended for our lives on this earth, and it leaves in its wake a destructive fallout that can permeate generations.

Everyone is interested in hearing about sex, but few will line up to hear about sin. Yet behind the glossy magazine covers and glamorous advertising, offstage from the television programs and films that tout casual sex as socially acceptable and personally enhancing, the damage caused by sexual sin to the human personality is more widespread than can hardly be imagined unless you have occasion to deal with that damage, as people in pastoral ministry do. I've witnessed the splintering that happens in the personalities of people who have been seduced into believing that "sex sin" is an old-fashioned oxymoron. As a pastor, and as someone who loves people, I hurt for those who have been deceived into believing the lie that they will find their true fulfillment and unleash their creative potential through the indiscriminate exercise of their sexuality.

In fact, the pop terminology for promiscuity today is "sexually active"—a de facto announcement that the lack of sexual activity reflects a passive, uninvolved-in-real-life person. On the other hand, being sexually active is made to define the alive, the vibrant, the knowledgeable and the fulfilled. The dishonesty of the whole thought structure and the social disapproval inherent in this terminology becomes a built-in pressure to concede to sexual activity as a verification of one's personhood. However, the hundreds of tragic stories I have heard in my lifetime from those who have fallen prey to this lie testify otherwise.

I have written this book to help people understand what the

Word of God has to say not only about sexual sin but also about healthy sexual fulfillment. God's joyous, creative intent in endowing humankind with sexuality is in sharp contrast to the portrayal of cheap, meaningless sex that bombards our culture, distorts our discernment and undermines our moral footing. Many people may be surprised to hear this fact asserted: *God invented sex*, but He did so on *His* terms. Sex isn't a subject to be either embarrassed about or ashamed of, but it is one to pursue in the light of the maker's wisdom and plan for sexual fulfillment.

God confronts us at the point of our sexual practices—at the center of our potential for life's highest physical satisfaction. And He does so with a list of rules, but not because He objects to our being happy or fulfilled. To the contrary, Father God, our creator, tells us in the Bible—the "owner's manual" He has provided us—how to handle life and what things are dangerous or self-destructive. Like any good parent, He warns His beloved children, "Don't do these things or you will hurt yourself."

Some time ago, I delivered a series of teachings to our congregation at The Church On The Way on the topic of "Ex-Rated Sex." I called it "Ex-" (rather than "X-"), because I was dealing with sexual values that had become labeled passé in our society ("ex"-values—i.e., "former" values; values no longer considered relevant). The problem that ex-values pose is that once we discard the timeless moral standards taught in the Word of God, people end up reaping the terrible harvest of the fruit of their sin. It's a bitter harvest never intended by the creator of our marvelous capacity for sexual fulfillment and one the world is generally unwilling to acknowledge until it's too late.

Another generation has risen up since I began to teach on this subject—a subject I've dealt with candidly and compassionately since I began ministry as a college youth pastor over 40 years ago. However, the changes in practice are not what is so different today; rather, it is the public nature of the proposition that sexual indulgence is no big deal anymore—no matter how perverse, how promiscuous or how painful the consequences. Through the years I have witnessed victims of our altered worldview on sex continue to reel in confusion and suffering amid the debris of a sexual revolution. Desensitized and debauched sexuality pervades every arena of public life—the media and the marketers rely upon sexual images and sexual misinformation to attract our attention, get our money and, in the process, offer the enemy of our souls a clear shot at hooking us into bondage.

The truth is not that society is more sinful today than at other times in history; the truth is that this is surely the most *deadly* time in humankind. Since the beginning of the HIV/AIDS epidemic, nearly 22 million people have died of AIDS; and as of the start of 2004, more than 43 million lives had been legally aborted in the United States alone.[1] These numbers stagger the mind and rival the death toll of terrorist attacks or wars.

There are 10 reasons why sex sins are worse than other sins. Five of those reasons have to do with the damage that results in the souls of people who engage in sexual sin, and the other five have to do with the collateral damage that takes place on the people (and the world) around us. Like a mushroom cloud billowing out from an atomic explosion, the spread of fallout from sexual sin registers its impact beyond the privacy of the person or persons sinning—polluting families, compromising character in the workplace or in the community, and wounding the Body of Christ.

The Word of God declares, "none of us lives to himself, and no one dies to himself" (Rom. 14:7), putting forever to rest society's pathetic notion that by engaging in sex sin, "I'm not hurting anyone but myself." This is especially argued when it comes to solo sex sins such as masturbation and pornography: "It's nobody's business but mine!" But sexual sin becomes as toxic, as invasive, as hereditary, as transferable and as ruinous as cancer. The Bible provides both warnings and case histories to evidence the damaging consequences of sexual indulgence, disobedience to God's laws and irresponsible behavior upon others, not just upon oneself.

Sin is a drastic issue, and whether or not one feels guilty about it isn't a gauge of its destructiveness. Guilt is a reality engraved in the moment of the event, not merely a feeling a person has about his or her actions. Guilt is not only an attitude held by the sinner but also a label for the impact of sin. We cannot commit sin of any kind without something being thrown awry, which eventually and inevitably will bring collapse. The whole realm of human sexuality must be seen in light of a disintegrating culture that knows nothing of the Word of God and that walks in its own lusts and passions; a society which, living in its own bondage, relentlessly pleads its own righteousness.

Amid this, it is not God's heart to condemn as much as it is to *restore, redeem* and to extend the *forgiveness* and release that Jesus reveals, just as He did toward the woman caught in the act of sexual sin. Our Savior leads us toward a new capacity to live life *as it was meant to be*. Yet as gracious and loving as Jesus is, He did not say to the woman (as a blinded society would argue), "Don't feel too bad about it, honey; we're all just human."

Forgiving the woman, Jesus said, *"Neither do I condemn you"*— an assertion that judgment was not coming down on her. And then He added, *"Go and sin no more"* (John 8:11, emphasis added). It was more than a command: Jesus' words are filled with *power*. They contain within them the spiritual strength and ability to make it possible for us to fulfill any summons, as long as it is our desire to do His will. Whether it's to make us triumphant over sin, to break the yoke of a past habit or bondage, or to bring us peace in the face of a present trial, Jesus is the living Word. When He comes to *live* in us who have truly invited Him in to dwell— to stay and take control—the things He says begin to *work* in our lives. Otherwise, without Him, we are sadly limited in moral fiber—helpless and without defense against either the lethal blows of our adversary or the brutal condemnation of his accusations.

My purpose in writing this book is to fortify hearts with an understanding of why God is so clear in His Word about calling us away from sexual sin, as well as to provide understanding about His commands to us regarding the proper and intended exercise of the sexual capacities He has so beautifully created and lovingly granted us. Contrary to the suppositions that many people have about the Christian view of human sexuality, we need not feel any hesitation in celebrating it—its privileges, its joys and its overwhelming fulfillment. But this celebration only sustains when our sexuality abides by the guidelines of His created order. Toward that goal, help can be found at the end of each chapter in the form of self-examination and prayers to minister hope and healing.

As we begin this book together, my objective is not to stand in condemnation regarding sex sins but rather to offer a pathway to deliverance, liberty and peace; and to clarify thinking in the midst of a sorely confused and deeply wounded society.

May God bless you as you read, either in receiving that grace for yourself or in ministering it to others.

ACKNOWLEDGMENTS

It is always with a sense of indebtedness that I complete any of my books, because I am so aware of my dependence upon people who make them possible.

I have no apology to make—as though I didn't really write this book—because I am deeply involved in communicating, from my heart to the reader's, with integrity and sincerity about sexual integrity. However, I have been efficiently and magnanimously served by gifted editorial assistance.

Selimah Nemoy is the God-given "right hand of blessing" He has granted for this project. I first met Selimah shortly after I became her pastor, when she wrote to me of a miraculous answer to her prayers and the amazing reunion of her family. I came to know her also as a result of her warm friendship with my mother. Nearly a decade later, she was employed by our lead administrator at The King's College and Seminary and assigned the task of overseeing our website.

Since that time, her skill has been manifest in her ability to distill hundreds of my sermons into practical formatting for download by users around the world. As I became aware of this happy occurrence—usually via e-mails from across the nation and the world—I was, at the same time, asked by my friends at Regal Books to pursue this multivolume project on sexual integrity. I knew that I could only achieve it with skilled, godly, discerning help.

So, my wife, Anna, and I both extend our thanks to Selimah. She has blessed us with her devotion to duty—not only laboring on this manuscript, but also maintaining her responsibilities at The King's simultaneously.

"The Lord gave the word: great was the company of those

that published it" (Ps. 68:11, *KJV*). Selimah Nemoy and Regal Books are among the great company of people who permit people like me to have the privilege of serving you, the reader, in this way. Thank the giver for that—He is God Almighty, the always good and gracious One.

Jack W. Hayford
Pastor, The Church On The Way
Chancellor, The King's College and Seminary

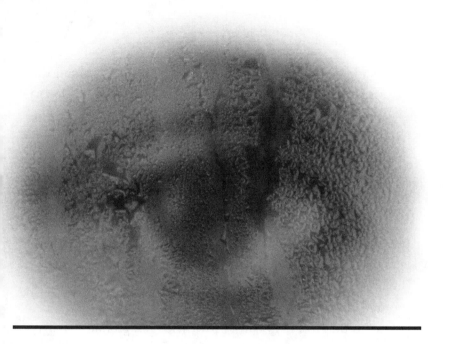

CHAPTER ONE

CAN WE TALK?

It is impossible to talk about sex and not be direct, candid and forthright at every point; but my experience in Christian circles has at times suggested that such candor is unwelcome. I offer no excuse or justification for the prudishness that has often cluttered clear communication among "the holy," but rather I have sought to tear down the barricades to simple honesty in communication—often using humor (getting us to laugh at ourselves)—without being either tawdry, cheap or irreverent.

In opening seminars or sermons I've presented on God's Word and human sexuality, I've often related the following story clipped out of a newspaper decades ago.

A middle-aged and intensely modest woman was planning to spend her summer vacation with her husband at a campground in the South. Not wanting to arrive unprepared, she wrote a letter to the campground manager inquiring about the lavatory facilities. When she wrote the word "toilet" in the letter, it seemed too bold to her intense sense of propriety. So she changed "toilet" to the old-fashioned term "bathroom commode." Still feeling that was too bold, she decided to abbreviate it and simply use the letters "BC." What she wrote was "Does the campground have its own BC?"

When the campground manager read that sentence, he had no idea what the woman was talking about. He showed it to some other people, and they couldn't figure it out either. Finally, he decided that she must be asking about whether the campground had its own *Baptist Church*.

With that in mind, here is what the campground manager wrote back.

Dear Madam,

I regret very much the delay in answering your letter, but I now take the pleasure of informing you that a BC is located nine miles north of the campground. And it is capable of seating 250 people at a time. I admit that is quite a distance away if you are in the habit of going regularly, but no doubt, you will be pleased to know that a great number of people take their lunches along and make a complete day of it. They usually arrive early and stay late. The last time my wife and I went was six years ago. It was so crowded we had to stand up the whole time. I would say, it pains me not to go more often, but it is surely no lack of desire on my part. However, as we grow older, it seems to be more of an effort. If you do decide to come down to our campground, perhaps I could go with you the first time. I'd be glad to sit with you and introduce you to all the other people. We want you to know this is a friendly campground.

I've shared that exchange of letters around the world and never found an audience that didn't laugh hilariously—or at least get the point. It's a humorous and useful lesson in what happens when we are not clear, direct and forthright, and how confusing speech can become when we aren't totally candid. And I share this story to prepare you, since I want to speak frankly—neither religiously nor crudely, but bluntly and pointedly—on the subject of sex.

Neither "God" nor "sex" are four-letter words.

Neither "God" nor "sex" are four-letter words, yet this discussion has always been subject to a number of hindering myths: that sex is fundamentally sinful (it isn't), that the fall of humankind was due to sex (it wasn't) and that prudishness equals holiness (it doesn't). Do you think God was surprised when He saw Adam and Eve rustling in the bushes and declared, "How awful! What have I done?"

These hindering myths have been promoted by the silence of the pulpit—a silence often reinforced by teaching that the virgin birth was necessary because intercourse is essentially sinful even within marriage and, among some traditions, that the priesthood should be celibate because deep devotion, or fullest holiness, is impossible to those who engage in sexual love. This silence, at times, has resulted in some of the worst cases of sexual sin; ignoring our sexuality will never lead us to freedom—truth about it will. As Jesus Himself said, "You shall know the truth, and the truth shall make you free" (John 8:32). The absence of truth, clarity and gracious instruction lends itself to an atmosphere conducive to bondage—either the bondage of rebellion against distortion or the bondage of an unrealistic view of our humanness.

WHY IS THE PULPIT SO SILENT?

The issue of sex is too seldom addressed by spiritual leaders, other than by occasional bland superficial comment or sporadic blasting condemnation. This reticence isn't so much because of embarrassment but because of the potential awkwardness of the theme. No leader wants to fumble words with such a delicate subject as sex, to stumble into appearing either naïve or unduly knowledgeable or to communicate a heavy-handed, guilt-inducing spirit of condemnation. Faithful leaders don't want to be misunderstood about the biblical imperative on sexual purity; and it's easier to presume that people know what's right and wrong than it is to thread through the myriad questions and problems that surface when the subject is addressed.

Further, pulpits are sometimes silent on the subject of sex because of the leader's own past personal fracture or wound—even a point of personal bondage in his or her own private life. My wife, Anna, and I have counseled hosts of spiritual leaders who have had sexual difficulties and unhappiness in their own marriages. Their emotions and conflicts about sex removed any base of comfort or confidence to address the subject from the platform, even though they're now walking in purity and fidelity themselves. When a married couple, devoted as servant partners in God's kingdom, have not learned how to healthily relate to one another sexually, the subject cannot be addressed effectively to others. Silence or blandness prevails, and a flock goes unfed in this fundamental area of needed understanding in the human experience. It is a double hook of the adversary's bondage, crippling the full release of a leader's potential in both ministry and marriage.

While a healthy, fulfilling biblical attitude toward sex may need more discussion in churches, the unfortunate message that *has* begun to seep through has been the seeming normalization of moral failure. From leaders to those being led, the ensuing confusion regarding biblical morality is abundantly apparent. The twisting of Scriptures to make room for any number of sexual sins is nothing new, but today we are watching sexual sin become accepted even by Christians—believers who have not been taught anything else. Within the Church today we find casual notions about masturbation and mutual gratification without intercourse, debasing practices demanded by married men of their wives and even a softening of conviction regarding whether homosexuality is really wrong or if God, in fact, created some people as homosexuals.

In response to the ignorance and acceptance of sexual sin by many Christians, Focus on the Family recruited a team of Bible scholars—the Council on Biblical Sexual Ethics—to develop a Bible-based statement on sexual behavior. I am one of the signers endorsing the "Colorado Statement on Biblical Sexual Morality," a declaration I see as a significant contribution to undoing the confusion caused by silence in our churches. To abolish in yourself the hindering myth that sex is of itself a sinful, shameful subject for discussion, read the council's full statement (see appendix 4).

WHY AM I TALKING ABOUT SEX?

Notwithstanding the high-profile cases of moral failure on the part of a few spiritual leaders, the vast majority of men and women I have met in public ministry are deeply committed, godly people. Still, relatively few say very much about the subject of our sexuality, its God-designed, enriching purposes and the wisdom He gives for avoiding its pollution, destructiveness or perversion.

So, why am I talking about it? That's a good question. Many times I've asked that question myself: "Why me, Lord?" For over four decades, I've been invited to teach and speak in conferences in virtually every kind of setting and to every age group—from teens and collegians to adult singles and marrieds. On campuses and in churches, I am still urged to speak, as I have for years from my own pulpit, on the subject of sex. I've concluded that perhaps the Lord has given me an ability and grace to communicate the Word of God regarding His blessing of sex and the destructive bane of its misappropriation. It is a special privilege to serve in helping people toward God's freeing truth on this topic. I don't feel prideful or smug about it, but I know it is part of my assignment under His Word's authority.

Two factors have enabled me to speak with real confidence and boldness on the subject of why sex sins are worse than others. The first is that by the grace of God—and I want to underscore that it is *by the grace of God*—I have been kept pure in my sexual life for a lifetime. I honor Jesus Himself, thanking my Lord that though my sexual life has certainly not gone unchallenged by temptation, He has enabled me to maintain purity. This has contributed greatly to my sense of freedom and boldness to speak on this subject.

But a second factor cannot be overlooked, for it also enables me to communicate with pastoral and personal authority. I have been blessed to know the high fulfillment of having been joined to only one person for my entire life—my dear wife, Anna. Our relationship has required a lifetime of growth, but our relationship has been in fidelity and purity, and always with the genuine joy that God intended for marriage's sexual union.

To those who might ask, "Well, if you have never failed in sexual transgression, how are you able to understand people who have?" I would respond that I am able to because (1) I know my own capacity for failure and have no illusions about being superior to others, even though I have kept pure; and (2) I do understand people's *capacity* for failure. After you have dealt with a few hundred people who, out of human vulnerability and brokenness, have failed, you learn a little bit about failure—and about the path to recovery and health.

WHO AM I TALKING TO?

First, it's important to make clear that in discussing why sex sins are worse than other sins, I am primarily addressing the subject as I would with people who have already made a commitment to Jesus Christ. I don't mean to imply that the truth that sex sins are worse than other sins is any less valid for some people, but rather that it can be misunderstood to suggest that those guilty of sexual sin are more offensive to God than others. They aren't, and I want to make that clear. But my presumed audience is essentially those who have already received Christ as Savior and who want His Lordship and purpose in *all* of their lives—including in their sexual behavior.

Everyone reading these words is the same as I am: We are sinners who need a Savior. The meaning of "sin" is not difficult to understand: it is what we do when we transgress God's will and His ways—His benevolently given laws. In this regard, the Bible says that to transgress in one respect is to become guilty of the whole of God's law (see Jas. 2:10), which is why every person is invited to appeal to God's immense offer of mercy, grace and forgiveness through His Son.

Because you have opened this book, you are clearly interested in dealing with issues of the heart—you are clearly serious about confronting anything that could be destructive to or disruptive of knowing a life of fulfillment and purpose. And if you have not until now opened yourself to God's love through the gift of His Son, I can only encourage you to do so as soon as you are willing to make that decision. It may be now—or perhaps as you continue reading—that you will come to a more definitive willingness to recognize both the need and the wisdom to open yourself to the Savior's life, grace, joy and hope.

A pivotal need for both you and me is the need to *repent*—that is, to turn away from our sins. You may feel you lack the power to do this, which is why the Bible says we need to call on the Lord to save us. Like dying or drowning people, we need the Son of God—Jesus Himself—who died for us and rose again: He is able to save us, to forgive us and to give us new life. So when you are willing to take that step with Him, remember, "Whoever calls on the name of the LORD [Jesus] *shall be saved*" (Rom. 10:13, emphasis added)! To help you do that, we have placed a prayer for personal salvation in appendix 1. I sincerely pray that you will seek salvation in Christ today—*now*, at this beginning point, since you are obviously open and inquiring about how to become a person who avoids the destructive and who takes constructive steps forward. The best first steps are toward God and His purposes for your life—beginning with receiving His Son as your Savior.

This is a book that targets people who care about God's ways. Your interest in the subject of sexual integrity may be for any number of reasons: you work with youth; you counsel people in your church; you've struggled with temptation; you've failed but are seeking to establish your ways in God's wisdom;

you are a student with an honest mind, seeking to know right and to live righteously.

Foundational to the matter of sexual integrity, however, is taking seriously both the gift of our humanness and the choices that clear-minded stewardship of our bodies requires in the light of God's freeing, fulfilling truth. This involves the issue of *discipleship*. It is one thing to believe in Jesus and trust Him as your Savior; it is quite another to follow Him as an obedient disciple, acknowledging Him as Lord. In either case, whether we are new believers or growing disciples, God's Word speaks pointedly about how we use our bodies.

- We worship with our bodies: "Present your bodies a living sacrifice, holy, acceptable to God, which is your reasonable service" (Rom. 12:1).
- Our bodies are the Holy Spirit's temple: "Do you not know that your body is the temple of the Holy Spirit?" (1 Cor. 6:19).
- We are not to defile this physical temple of God (see 1 Cor. 3:16-17).
- As believers, we will be held specifically accountable for "the things done in the body" (2 Cor. 5:10).

Those truths combine to bring a demanding point to bear on every person who is serious about God, serious about His gift to us in His Son, Jesus Christ, and who seriously cares about other people.

WE WILL FACE A SOBERING REALITY

A surprising number of Christians are ignorant of the fact that *we will stand before the Lord Jesus for an evaluative judgment*—an ultimate accounting—for how we have lived and served as followers of Him. Though all people will stand before God's great white throne of ultimate judgment, the Bible reveals in Revelation 20:11-15 that only the unbelieving—only those refusing God's way of life in His Son—will be judged for their sins. We believers can be very thankful that we won't be judged for our sins, since the shame and penalty of our sins were swallowed up through Jesus' death on the cross. However, we still will face a sobering reality.

When we stand before the Lord, the quality of our motives, thoughts and actions will be tested by fire—discerning and revealing what each of us has done with our lives as believers.

> For no other foundation can anyone lay than that which is laid, which is Jesus Christ. Now if anyone builds on this foundation with gold, silver, precious stones, wood, hay, straw, each one's work will become clear; for the Day will declare it, because it will be revealed by fire; and the fire will test each one's work, of what sort it is (1 Cor. 3:11-13).

As the following passage shows us, we will not be *saved by* our works, but we will answer to how we have *served* our master *with* our works—and specific mention is made to the way we regard our bodies as *His gift to us for His glory*.

> Therefore we make it our aim, whether present or absent, to be well pleasing to Him. For we must all appear before the judgment seat of Christ, that each one may receive the things done in the body, according to what he has done, whether good or bad (2 Cor. 5:9-10).

There is nothing about this that smacks of "salvation by works," because the issue here has nothing to do with being saved. But there is a very sobering reality in view—especially when we come to the issues we believers face if we are going to follow Jesus Christ through a world filled with darkened minds and a perverted concept of human sexuality. While full forgiveness is secured for *every sin* we bring to the Cross, and while full righteousness is conferred upon us through faith alone as we put our trust in Christ, we will still be called to stand before Jesus to give account for our use of His gift of life to us. The joy of reward awaits faithful disciples; the reality of losing our reward is too seldom considered. If our works, as servants of Christ, are wood, hay and straw, they will be consumed by fire. And although we will suffer the loss of our reward for faithful stewardship of our lives, we will still be saved. Yet serious discipleship calls us to integrity and purity, devotion to Jesus and delight in doing His will—basic goals for our entire lives.

Few things in our world are more taunting or tempting, distracting or distorting, than the siren song that summons us toward sexual promiscuity, sexual indulgence or casual attitudes about sex. It is by no means an accident that the Bible describes the spirit of this world as both the Antichrist and the mother of harlots (see 1 John 4:3; Rev. 17:5). Spiritual compromise and sexual compromise go hand in hand throughout all of God's Word, as they do in the pragmatic details of daily life.

So, let us set forward to examine *Fatal Attractions: Why Sex Sins Are Worse Than Others.* And just as we opened with humor, to laugh out of the room any notion that we will be less than candid, we conclude our introductory lesson with sobriety, to press from our hearts any notion that we dare be less than serious about our commitment.

Building a life of sexual integrity is worth the discipleship it costs. It is a lifestyle we can all be energized to attain by God's power as we open ourselves to the fullness of His Holy Spirit. He has promised this dynamic enablement not only to keep us faithful and to bring us "before the presence of His glory with exceeding joy" (Jude 24) but also to help us grow a life of healthy sexual fulfillment. Such health can bring strength and stability in our own lives, as well as equip us to help others navigate today's storms of sexual confusion.

To gain focus, then, and to bring biblical clarity and health to our thinking about our sexuality as disciples of Jesus, let's proceed. There are many reasons why sex sins are worse than others, beginning with the tragic impact of sexual sin on our sense of personhood—our identity as individuals.

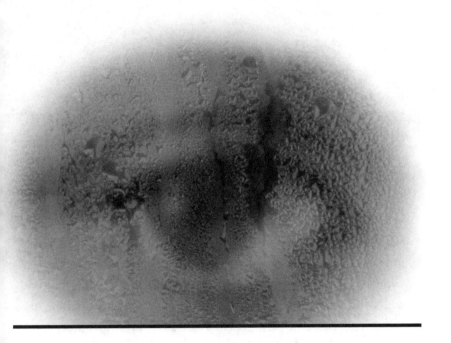

CHAPTER TWO

SEX SINS STAIN THE ROOT OF AN INDIVIDUAL'S IDENTITY

If the foundations are destroyed, what can the righteous do?
PSALM 11:3

The first and foundational reason why sex sins are worse than others is because sex sins stain the root of an individual's identity.

It had taken a while to pull the story out of her, but now Edie sat on a chair across from me, her long brown hair spilling over her shoulders as she wept in embarrassment and shame.[1] So deeply had she buried the memory of being molested by her brother that she'd nearly convinced herself it hadn't happened. Even worse, perhaps, Edie had gone on to rationalize that her teenaged brother's violation of her when she was only five years old didn't really matter. She told me she'd forgiven him, but the fact was, she'd never really dealt with the damage.

It had been 30 years since Edie's trust was betrayed and her self-esteem destroyed in an old shed at the far end of a neighbor's backyard. A demand of silence on the part of her brother—whom she adored—sealed Edie to a lifetime of believing that in order for people to love her, she had to let them hurt her. At puberty, she quickly became sexually active, and as an adult, Edie suffered one failed relationship after another, coming to believe that she wasn't worth loving, perhaps even that life wasn't worth living. She is a study in one proven fact: Sex sins—more than any other sin—corrupt an individual's primary sense of identity.

In the raw physiological facts of life, there is nothing so fundamental to our personhood as our genitals. When I was born, the doctor didn't say, "Oh, look. It's Jack." My name was added later. But the first way in which any of us was identified was either "It's a boy" or "It's a girl"—a fact that is far more deeply related to our whole sense of who we are than most of us are willing to acknowledge. You don't have to have been a counselor of broken humanity very long to recognize the deep sense of loss and isolation that occurs when the foundation of a person's identity is violated by sexual pollution.

At our innermost core, it is written in the human heart to recognize that kind of violation when it first occurs. Most of us can remember our earliest experience of some form of sexual disobedience, which at first, may have seemed stimulating and exciting. But how quickly and sharply it turned to bewilderment and shame. It happens in so many ways: to the blossoming young woman who allows herself to be fondled for the first time and to the young boy who begins to masturbate. Both are imprinted in their own ways by the arc of explosive self-discovery, which ends in humiliation and guilt.

It's not that everyone has willfully engaged in sexual immorality. But in a world of sin, compounded in its spread by a society void of moral values, we have been harmed in one way or another by the impact of sexual sin upon our lives. And we recognize it at the beginning. Notice is served from the first—before our consciences are seared through by recurrent acts—that the root of our identities has been touched in an inappropriate way, and we begin to feel a sense of loss—a shattering, a straining—as the very foundation of who we are has been shaken and violated.

CHILDHOOD SEXUAL ABUSE

The initial point of damage to a person's identity and the ensuing bondage that takes place happen, for most people, in their childhood. This may sound like an exaggeration, but let me assert it: Everyone is sexually abused in childhood! I don't necessarily mean by molestation or incest, though I've found there is more of that in the world than I ever dreamed I would encounter when I prepared for public ministry.

The primary form of sexual abuse I'm talking about is the abuse of *too little or aimless training*. This opens up the whole arenas of what you were taught as a child and now, as an adult, how you teach your children about sex. Generally, there is an unwillingness on the part of parents to accept responsibility to talk to their kids about sex, and then, if they do, too often it is with an approach that is too timid or too permissive or too authoritarian or too prudish. Such communication becomes ineffective—stifling the intended purpose, because it seems irrelevant and out of sync with the culture or is presented with insufficient reasoning to legitimize the Bible's worldview.

We need to talk sensibly to our children about sex as soon as any interest or curiosity about their sexuality first expresses itself. Further, we need to take our guidelines from the Word of God. Some handbooks will tell you that when a baby sits in the tub and explores his or her sex organs, enjoying pleasurable feelings, it's only natural. But what the handbooks never bother to say is that human beings in their "natural" state are fallen.

Like virtually every child does, Anna's and my kids had a natural tendency to explore themselves, and we had to deal with that. This happens normally with all children, at bathing time for example, and just needs to be dealt with in simplicity—without shock and with carefulness to avoid creating an unusual atmosphere around the subject. The best way to understand sin in a child is the same way you understand their teeth. A little baby doesn't have much of a bite yet, but just give them a little time, and those teeth are going to surface and begin operating. Sin is present in all children—just as it is present in all human beings—and neglecting to address it early opens the door for possible damage to their souls.

Cultivating fears about sex is another form of abuse that can damage the health of a child's identity and taint his or her future fulfillment in marriage. It is often formed in girls by their mothers who, for one reason or another, are frightened of their own sexuality. The mother's fear of men creates a bondage point in her daughter's life so that when the daughter grows up, she cannot participate in the fullness of sexual possibility within her marriage.

Sexual violation experienced in childhood can also have a devastating effect upon a man's or a woman's capacity for healthy sexuality within marriage. An otherwise happily married Christian couple came to me for counseling many years ago because it seemed that the wife had lost all interest in their sexual relationship. As we prayed together, the Lord revealed an incident that had happened to this woman when she was 11 or 12 years old and her body was developing. She'd gone to a pool party at a relative's house and went into a little bathhouse to change into her swimming suit. As she was standing there nude, getting ready to put on her suit, the door opened, and an uncle stepped in. He stood there and leered at her, and then he said one word: "Nice." In that single moment, an innocent, vulnerable young girl was violated by a demon of lust that shot out of the man's eyes. Decades later, it was affecting her marriage.

THE TRAP OF CHILDHOOD SEXUAL SIN

There are *sexual sins* that happen among children. Little kids at play go into a side room or a garage or behind bushes, and in such moments seeds of long-term harm can be sown, even in the relative innocence of their talk, fumblings and inquiring actions. While no actual passion or sexual interchange may take place, first encounters do register negatively in their souls. Contemporary psychology may assert the opposite, but my own pastoral counseling has verified that even then, the child felt, *Something about this is wrong.* It can be the result of a compromise, when they sensed that what they were doing wasn't right but they did it anyway, and out of this comes a snare of bondage.

The Bible says that *fear creates a snare, or a trap* (see Prov. 29:25). Satan will take the fact that two little boys on a single occasion briefly touched one another's genitals, and from that one encounter, he leverages the proposition that thereby the now-grown men are homosexual. Then, if either of those men should ever feel even a noble affection for another man, the accuser's lie will press the point: "See! You are!" It is such early sins, invading childhood's innocence, that beget a distinct vulnerability to satanic deception. This deception comes in the form of lies that become convincing in the light of a distant memory and under the force of the hook—the snare that was set in place long before. In these ways, the enemy of our souls capitalizes on reaching back to that trap that was set for you when you were a child, and uses against you all the guilt, worthlessness and condemnation you feel.

DELIVERANCE FROM THE TRAP

When I met Mike, he'd just landed his first big role in a major motion picture, and he was engaged to be married. Endowed with movie-star good looks, Mike's features seemed to have been sculpted from a piece of fine marble. Over the years I knew him, he was a devoted disciple of Jesus Christ and a servant of the Lord. But the victory in his life had been hard-won.

An unusually handsome young boy, Mike had been mercilessly taunted by other children who'd called him the vulgar and cruel spectrum of names for a homosexual. Though Mike wasn't homosexual, as he grew from boyhood into puberty, fear and shame began to multiply in his soul. He was drawn first to masturbation and then, finally, seduced by an older boy into the homosexuality he so feared. Once Mike had pushed beyond the limits of his own moral register, his new lifestyle seemed liberating. He felt certain this was who he was meant to be, and the deception was reinforced by a new set of friends who defined themselves (and Mike) by their own rules. For the first time, Mike told me, he felt like he *belonged*; but the power of God's love was about to manifest in a way that would bring him a revelation of what belonging was truly about.

The prayers of Mike's mother had followed him for years. She had never rejected him, though he knew she had never approved of his sexual confusion either. When his day of deliverance began to dawn, Mike recognized that the living God was calling him back. The turnaround took place while he was sitting in a bar—secure in his professional success and the many friends he had who shared the lifestyle he was leading. Suddenly, an inner consciousness shook him to his core: *If you keep living this way, you're going to die.* Mike sat there, stunned by the sudden and unmistakable realization that the man he'd become was a person destined for ruin.

The entire story of Mike's full restoration is too lengthy to relate here, but the point it illustrates is how destructively early sexual violation can imprint a person's identity. The wrongness of that imprint led Mike into confusion about his manhood and into perversion in his expression of it. As Mike's true personality sought to emerge in his adulthood, the superficial feelings of success he seemed to enjoy were far from the fulfillment of his deepest hopes and dreams. Mike's repentance in turning to the Lord set in motion a viable and certain pathway toward recovery. He first discovered the confidence that comes from God's immediate and complete forgiveness, and progressively he began the process of letting the Holy Spirit peel back the accumulated debris of lies and confusion. By the time I met him, his eyes sparkled with clarity and peace.

Once the foundation of an individual's basic point of identity has been shaken, there comes a sense of uprootedness—a removal from life's source in God's gifts and life's fulfillment in

God's purpose. An entire lifetime can be crippled, and a hopeful future can progressively disintegrate when one's identity is polluted by sexual sin. To define ourselves in terms other than those the creator has conceived for us will inevitably bring a proportional distortion of everything about our lives.

> An entire lifetime can be crippled, and a hopeful future can progressively disintegrate when one's identity is polluted by sexual sin.

The tarnish that marked Mike's life—as well as Edie's—happened as a result of sexual violation and sexual sin, distorting their recognition of who they were meant to be. They stand as eroded-but-now-restored monuments to two realities: (1) what sex sin can do to taint a person's identity, and (2) what God's grace can do to recover and renew true identity through Christ.

Perhaps you or someone you know is haunted by staining shame, like Mike or Edie was. If so, take heart, because the Word of God declares that there is hope and healing available. The starting point for deliverance of any kind is to *examine oneself* (see 1 Cor. 11:28). All who are facing the damage caused by sexual impurity need to be willing to look honestly and openly at those places in their lives that have been polluted and broken, whether by actions of their own choice or because of violation by another. Painful as that process may be, no healing can be possible without an examination of the wound and removal of anything under the surface that is not life giving.

Second, the Lord invites us to "come boldly to the throne of grace, that we may obtain mercy and find grace to help in time of need" (Heb. 4:16). To assist you in applying the truth and ministering answers for each specific point addressed in this book, you will find at the end of each chapter a helpful prayer for not only turning *to* the Lord but also for turning *over to* the Lord any residue of bondage or stain in exchange for the liberty, wholeness and purity that are rightfully ours through the sacrifice of our Lord and Savior Jesus Christ.

May God's grace attend you as you seek to receive or to minister His help unto hope and healing.

HELP UNTO HOPE AND HEALING

Therefore, if anyone is in Christ, he is a new creation; old things have passed away; behold, all things have become new.

2 CORINTHIANS 5:17

Examining Myself

Is there a sexual experience in my childhood that I have not wanted to look back on because its memory is so painful and humiliating? Do I sometimes do things to gain people's love because deep inside I really don't think I'm worth loving? Am I willing to admit any sexual abuse of children on my part?

Turning to the Lord in Prayer

Heavenly Father, thank You for declaring in Your Word that I am no longer defined by the sexual sin that once tainted my life, because I have been given new life in Jesus Christ. I ask You, Lord, to forgive me for my sins, and I forgive those who have sinned against me. I invite Your Holy Spirit to penetrate every darkened place in my soul, shining the light and life of Jesus Christ and forming Your identity in me. Lord Jesus, please bring healing and recovery into my relationships with others as I turn away from the things that have kept me bound and as I walk in the freedom for which Christ has made me free [see Gal. 5:1]. *In Your blessed name, I pray, amen.*

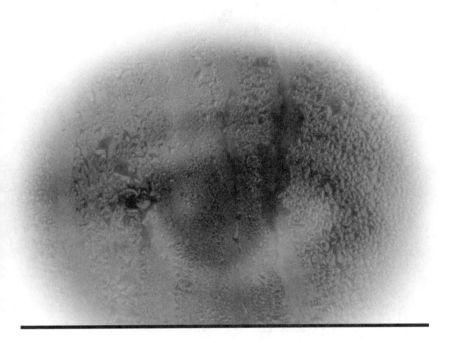

SEX SINS EXPLOIT THE DEEPEST ASPECTS OF OUR EMOTIONALITY

Can a man take fire to his bosom, and his clothes not be burned? Can one walk on hot coals, and his feet not be seared?

PROVERBS 6:27-28

Compounding the damage inflicted upon our identity, sex sins are worse than others because they exploit the deepest aspects of our emotionality. The following letter I received is indicative of the distortion and exploitation that sexual sin breeds.

Dear Pastor Jack,

My boyfriend, Donny, says that if God hadn't wanted for us to make love, He wouldn't let us feel the way we
do toward one another. Besides, the Bible says that perfect love casts out fear, so Donny says we shouldn't be
afraid to express our love to one another. I wanted to
wait till we were married to have sex, but he says as long
as we are truly in love, it isn't wrong. We've been together for five years, and I want so much to be his wife, but
we're young (I'm 25; he's 28), and Donny says we need
more time before taking the next step. I don't know how
much longer we should wait, and frankly, I'm just not
sure anymore if what we're doing is really okay with
God.

Lauren

Traps set by Satan in our childhood set us up for vicious
assaults as we enter the emotionally charged years of adolescence
and adulthood. Not only do they snare us in bondage, but also
they corrode our discernment and our ability to exercise wisdom. Cultural influences that come the way of young men and
women today promote sexual experience or experimentation as
a means of achieving fulfillment and acceptance, with marriage
and commitment generally reduced to a nearly irrelevant after-
thought—"if things work out." Movies, television, advertising,
the Internet and pop songs all contribute to a mythological and
warped perspective on human relationships and sexual behavior.
Even the lovely ballads my own generation enjoyed years
ago transmitted an element of demonic bondage in lyrics that

glorified enchantment (which is witchcraft) and romanticized the pain and suffering of brokenheartedness. Youth who feed on a world culture's diet of shallow fodder regarding sexual attitudes grow into emotionally ill-equipped adults, neutralized for discerning what qualities are worth cultivating in themselves (not to mention qualities of genuine and lasting value in others). When puberty strikes, young people are miserably unprepared to withstand the onslaught of destructive influences—social, educational, emotional and physiological—all of which too easily lead to sexual sin.

WE ARE CREATED IN THE IMAGE OF GOD

One key to the brokenness that figures prominently in the matter of surrendering to sexual sin is our perception of ourselves—more pointedly, we do not know who we are as creations in God's image. The priority of humankind's understanding this begins right at Genesis: "So God created man in His own image" (1:27). It is further underscored when our lives are redeemed through receiving the Savior, our Lord Jesus Christ, whom the Bible declares is "the express image" of God (Heb. 1:3) and to whose image we are "predestined to be conformed" (Rom. 8:29).

Through many years of pastoral counseling, it has become clear to me that with regard to sexual sin, both the seducer and the seduced are people whose personal and emotional identities are immature and not grounded in God's image. For that reason, they have readily fallen prey to misleading and false expressions of validation.

Since nothing is more emotionally or physically provocative than our sexuality, and since our society's restrictions on sex have essentially evaporated, the enemy of every soul uses sexuality as a means to further shred any sense of who we are. Sexual indulgence is deceitfully presented as a means to physically prove a person's worth (or prowess), emotionally violating those who are desperate to sense they deeply matter to other people and who yearn to feel loved. In fact, the entire appeal of the words "If you *really* loved me, you'd do it" are, in effect, a challenge. These words confront people who do not know what they "really" feel and present a demand that they prove themselves by sacrificing their own privilege of choice by surrendering to the will of their pursuer.

Individuals who are secure in their true identity—that is, people who are grounded in God's image of who they are—will not feel the need to prove themselves, either by increasing the number of notches of sexual experience they have on their belt or by allowing their personhood, values and body to be violated. While we may be identified by many characteristics of our lives—marital status, nationality, gifting or occupation—the only solid ground on which our identity can be secured and our self-image based is who we are in Jesus Christ.

Our world today is flooded with images that pressure people into the false notions that their identities are found in their physical bodies and that their acceptance and worth are measured by their sexual appeal. These are such fundamental lies that it almost seems unnecessary to address them; yet deep within the souls and minds of many people there is a brokenness in their emotional health that gives rise to these falsehoods, evidenced by the multimillions of dollars consumers spend to look or feel sexy. For those of us who have come to know Jesus Christ as our Lord and Savior, we have the authority to contend with this avalanche of untruth in that there is only one identity that holds fast: our identity in Jesus Christ through whom we are accepted by our Father God. As the old song goes, all the rest is sinking sand.

Contrary to the confusion about love that inundated Lauren (in contrast to the self-serving manipulation of her boyfriend, Donny), genuine love and relationship outside of marriage do not require sexual expression for fulfillment. Let me say that again: Genuine love and relationship outside of marriage do not require sexual expression for fulfillment. Even if they get married (though statistics aren't in their favor on that), Donny and Lauren's premarital violation of God's law has robbed them of experiencing the radical-to-our-society delight and high fulfillment of meeting as virgins upon the foundation of pristinely exchanged marriage vows. Sadly, this young couple is already a casualty of the world's false appeal.

> Genuine love and relationship outside of marriage do not require sexual expression for fulfillment.

EVERYONE WANTS TO BE LOVED

Our emotions are among the most powerful expressions of our souls and, as such, make us terribly vulnerable as human beings. There isn't a person alive who doesn't grow up wanting to be loved. Our human desire for love is a reflection of the depth of our heavenly creator's desire for and commitment to us. While virtually all people are conscious of desiring to be loved, the souls of countless men and women have been damaged by violation or bondage of the past. Consequently, their understanding about where and how to find fulfillment of this desire is too easily corrupted or confused. The saying "looking for love in all the wrong places" is a cliché—yet nothing could more accurately state the problem for so many. Beyond the gross and perverted expressions of relationship often presented as normal via media and pop philosophy, deep within every human soul there will forever be a longing for that *special one*—one who loves me as no other, who is solely devoted to me and to me alone. The changing landscape of our society has reduced the likelihood of whole and healthy family relationships, which supply the love that establishes security and identity in a person, the kind of love that will brace a soul against the pursuit of unworthy or abnormal relationships. Yet the human heart today is the same as it has always been—one designed by God to know His love, not only personally with Him, but also in pure relationships with others.

Contrary to the bill of goods that's been sold to society, breaking every sexual convention and taboo hasn't brought any of us more liberty—only more enslavement and brokenness. In the absence of knowing God's truth and wisdom on the subject, so many sincere minds are clouded with confusion. Many arrive at adulthood already in bondage, unable to navigate the wreckage left behind by the so-called sexual revolution. Seeking to find the genuine fulfillment for which every heart longs is a daunting task, even for believers in Jesus Christ.

As a pastor, I've been privileged to deal with hurting, wounded people who have become tangled in sexual sin—precious souls who have fallen prey to the deceit of false promises. Because sexual activity awakens our deepest passions, it also exposes us to the greatest risk of emotional violation and injury. At the center of her story, Lauren suffered the exploitation of every human being's deepest need for acceptance and love. The same was also true of Edie and Mike, whose stories were told in chapter 2. They gave themselves over to another person, sensing it was wrong but being overwhelmed by the vacuum in their own souls for love and a sense of belonging. To any so sorely tempted or bruised, the Word of God offers sound advice in defense of this most vulnerable and easily damaged facet of our human personality: "Keep your heart with all diligence" (Prov. 4:23). Tragically, however, that word is often heard too late.

I doubt there is a person living who doesn't know what a heart broken by betrayal or rejection feels like. This agony is compounded dozens of times over in the souls of people who are also engaged in sexual sin. The guilt taunts them. This is true not only of people outside Christ but also of those believers in Jesus Christ who, with the passing of years—finding themselves still unmarried—have been duped into compromising their purity. Sadly, the hoped-for gain turns to loss as they discover that what held a promise of relationship the night before has evaporated in the morning light. Such emotional pain is excruciating. Precious souls have not only been broken and scarred by individuals whom they thought were trustworthy but also bear the shame and distance they feel for having violated their commitments to the living God.

Sexual impurity not only kills off something in the ones who have been exploited but also maims the seducers as well. Manipulators like Donny become hard and jaded, increasingly less capable of experiencing true love and fulfillment themselves. In time, if the damage goes unattended, it compounds itself in future repetitive behavior and deteriorative attitudes in either or both parties. By rejecting, or never having been taught, the wisdom of God's fulfilling ways, both the seducers and the seduced will likely find themselves at an emotional dead end.

But please say a "Hallelujah!" with me: Our God is a glorious redeemer, fully able to recover and repair even the most damaged souls. He is ever ready to bring us wholeness in Jesus Christ and thereby lay a solid foundation for the future. With that, walls of defense may be built, enabling us to discern and to defend ourselves from the thieving tactics of our ferocious enemies—our weak selves and our strong adversary. There is no bondage He cannot untangle, no hurt He cannot heal. For those who long to be loved but have never known how, God's Holy Spirit not only can bring a sense of cleansing forgiveness through Jesus' cross but also will restore and rebuild the shattered temple of your soul and make it a glorious place for God's love to dwell.

HELP UNTO HOPE AND HEALING

Let us not love in word or in tongue, but in deed and in truth. And by
this we know that we are of the truth, and shall assure our hearts
before Him. For if our heart condemns us, God is greater than
our heart, and knows all things.
1 JOHN 3:18-20

Examining Myself
Have I allowed myself to be sexually exploited because I was afraid that no one would love me unless I did? Is there anyone in my life whom I've taken advantage of sexually but whom I haven't, until today, wanted to acknowledge? What alternatives to God's fulfilling love have I sought, to the frustration of my own goals and compromise of myself and other persons?

Turning to the Lord in Prayer

Lord, You know the beginning and the end of my days [see Rev.
1:8]. Forgive me for the times I have left wisdom behind and
followed the seducer of my soul to the door of emotional death.

I ask for forgiveness of those whom I have hurt, and I declare my forgiveness and release of those persons who have hurt me. I pray that Your Holy Spirit would enter into that now-empty place in my life and fill it with the wholeness of Your love and a passion for Your purity. I commit myself to walk in Your wisdom and Your way. In Jesus' name, amen.

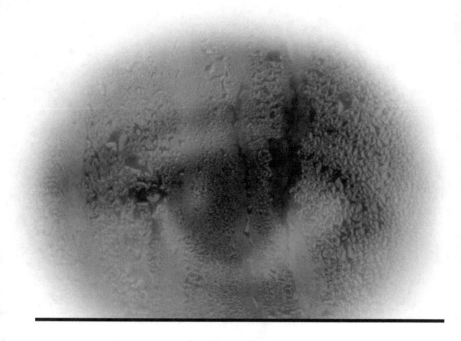

CHAPTER FOUR

SEX SINS POLLUTE THE FOUNTAINHEAD OF OUR HIGHEST CREATIVITY

The LORD God formed man of the dust of the ground, and breathed into his nostrils the breath of life; and man became a living being.
GENESIS 2:7

The third reason why sex sins are worse than others is because sex sins pollute the fountainhead of our highest creativity.

The Bible says that God created man in His own image and,

according to the literal Hebrew, breathed into him the breath o. *lives.* God has poured so much of His likeness and Person into us, including the awesome power to create life and to do so at will. Literally, under the creator's gift, we are able to give birth to *eternal beings.* As believers in Jesus Christ, we are called to stewardship of this life-giving ability. It is because we possess this God-given privilege to *beget life* that the adversary of our souls so viciously assails our sexuality. I am persuaded that his hate for humankind is partially related to our capacity to beget beings in the image of God (even though presently that image has been damaged).

The drama of the ages—the war between good and evil—is a struggle between God's will and Satan's wiles. In the middle is humankind, who all the time is increasing in number, either unto eternal gain or eternal loss. Fundamental to the outcome of this war is how many will be saved. So if our enemy can spoil life from its inception—if he can strike with corrupting impact the very begetting of lives—he will, and most certainly, he does so.

Further, as believers in Christ, not only do we have that God-given capacity to *beget* a human life, but also we have the responsibility to live in the disciplines to which Jesus calls us. These include living purely and faithfully in respect to our sexuality and in raising our children to know and love the Lord, thereby making radical gains in the number of those who will be saved.

BEGETTING SPIRITUAL INHERITANCE

Billy's parents went through a painful divorce when Billy was nine. His mother, who'd tried to raise him as a believer in Jesus Christ, had been devastated by her husband's infidelity. But Billy

and looked forward to the weekends he got to
Though occasionally there was a different
...is dad's house when Billy visited, she'd be left behind
as father and son went and did fun things together.

When Billy became an adolescent, sex was soon integrat-ed into his "recreation," with merely a warning by his dad to protect himself by using condoms. Yet as he grew into an adult, Billy found that he was never able to form wholesome, lasting relationships with women, nor anything more mean-ingful than competitive friendships with men. When his father's attention drifted away from his now grown son, Billy was lost.

Billy's story is not only an illustration—it is also a sad, sad picture repeated over and over millions of times around us. As parents, we contribute more than biological genes to our chil-dren; both our character and our actions affect either a *shield* of wisdom and godliness that protects them or a *shedding* of their wholeness and integrity that diminishes them, like the death that causes leaves to fall in autumn.

I do not want to bring condemnation upon anyone, nor is what I am about to say to you something I feel self-righteous about, but I do think it's important to be said. I am humbly glad before God that I am able to testify to each of my four children, "You are products of your mother's and my love for one anoth-er—love that was never compromised with anyone else. You were born through the enterprise of two bodies that, in their affection for one another, their commitment to one another and their union with one another, begot you as a pure human being. Whatever your imperfections, you did not enter through the gates of bodies that were soiled and tainted by involvement with others."

In my book *Blessing Your Children*, I write about the spiritual inheritance that we pass on to our children. Spiritual inheritance is as real as the DNA that determines our biological characteristics. Among the histories of people we read about in the Bible, the lives of Lot and David are filled with indisputable evidence as to why sex sins are so horribly damaging, not only to the person who commits them but also to the generations that follow. The Bible is God's Word, which gives us His laws about how we ought to live for maximum fulfillment as well as *history*, providing us documented evidence about how people no different from you or me submitted to sexual sin, bringing harm and suffering upon generations to come.

When we are born again in Jesus Christ, God plants His spiritual seed in us. How we nurture (or neglect) that seed determines three things: whether we will grow healthy or bent; whether we, as His disciples, will bear fruit; and whether that fruit will be sweet or bitter, wholesome or withered. Committing to *live* and *love* within our creator's laws and on our Savior's terms is a summons to which every believer is called to respond. As the adversary continues his heinous advance at so many points in our present world, carving destructive inroads with regard to human sexuality, we are wise to *receive* and *apply* the wisdom of God's truth to our lives.

Sins of all kinds—but particularly sex sins—poison us at the root of our identity, humanity and creativity. When we have been tainted by sin, growth in those aspects of our personhood is blocked or retarded. Health, life and effectiveness become reduced or withered; and if we do bear fruit, too often the fruit is either contaminated with something of the bittersweet of our failure, or it relays something less than nourishing to others.

God desires that we would see the meeting point between our spiritual and our physical capacities. If we do not learn the *discipline* of His ways in our sexual capacities (which are a part of His creative design in us), then we will never learn the *glory* of His creative capacity working through us in a spiritual dimension. The discipline of my life—begetting sexual capacities, according to God's order, not only brings tremendous fulfillment at a sexual level in my life but also releases me to become "new life"— begetting in the spiritual dimension of my life, as an instrument of the creative will of God.

> It's often the little burglaries that we let Satan get away with that lead to the wholesale robbery of all that matters to us.

Jesus tells us that the thief comes to steal, kill and destroy (see John 10:10). Tragically, it's often the little burglaries that we let him get away with that lead to the wholesale robbery of all that matters to us: that seemingly innocent flirtation on the Internet that destroys a marriage; the casual glancing at pornographic magazines on the news rack, which sends a man into the toilet stall; the halting pause on a cable TV station of sexual explicitness that surrenders a mind to the spirit of pornography when channel surfing. To stand our ground as disciples of the Lord Jesus Christ, it's imperative that we guard our hearts and minds; each of us is equally vulnerable to overlooking the "little" indiscretions that ultimately pollute the fountainhead of our highest creativity and transmit the heritage of that failure to our children.

HELP UNTO HOPE AND HEALING

Christ has redeemed us from the curse of the law, having become a curse
for us (for it is written, "Cursed is everyone who hangs on a tree").
GALATIANS 3:13

Examining Myself

How have I nurtured (or neglected) God's seed planted in me?
Are there children I know who are growing up "bent" because of
the sexual sins of their parents?

Turning to the Lord in Prayer

Lord God, in Jesus' name, I take authority over every demonic
thing that has attempted to invade my family and over the sin
that has given place to them; and I declare right now that by
the blood of Jesus they will claim no more dominion in our
lives. Where my sin has opened a door for Satan to harass my
children, I close it now; and by my actions, thoughts and
prayers from this day forward, I press toward the purity that
will allow Your seed to flourish in all of us. Thank You for Your
Kingdom power and the authority You have given to me
through the sacrifice of Your Son, Jesus Christ, and by His Holy
Spirit. I stand now as Your faithful disciple, growing straight
and growing strong in You, because of Your life in me
and through me to others. Amen.

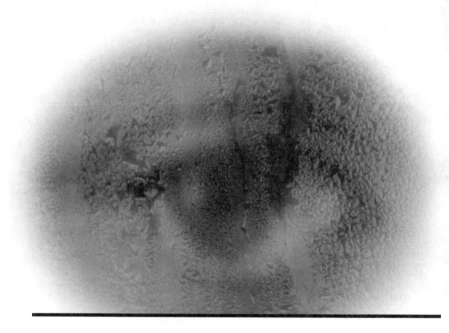

CHAPTER FIVE

SEX SINS PRODUCE GUILT THAT CRIPPLES CONFIDENCE AND AUTHORITY

Those who practice [the works of the flesh] will not inherit the kingdom of God.

GALATIANS 5:21

The next reason in our study of why sex sins are worse than others is that sex sins produce guilt that cripples confidence and authority. This is an issue that especially applies to every believer who desires to serve Christ—either in public ministry or ministry in one's sphere of influence.

Elliot was in his late 20s and appeared to have a bright future in ministry. He had written to my office in advance of a regional leadership conference and asked if I might set aside a few minutes to talk with him during my visit. He strongly sensed the Lord's call to reach out to the most damaged souls in the inner cities and had been offered an associate pastor's position at a nearby church. We met at my hotel's coffee shop for an early morning breakfast and sat in a back booth where we could speak privately.

"Pastor Jack," Elliot said, "I've trained a long time to be ready for this ministry opportunity, but there's something that yet has me hindered. I felt I could trust you with it.

"When I was a senior in college, there was this girl in one of my classes with whom I became study partners. It wasn't that she was such a knockout or that I was on the make, but we were just so in sync when it came to studying together. As the school year went on, we started meeting at football games, and then, finally, we began just getting together in the evenings, alone with one another—no books, no library, no stadium crowds—just to talk.

"I had fought temptation all through high school, even when the other guys were pressuring me to start 'acting like a man.' I never surrendered because I knew there was a call on my life to serve Jesus. But one night, alone with this girl to whom I felt so connected, every impulse I'd ever felt began to overwhelm me, and I kissed her. Suddenly, it was as if all the barriers had collapsed. We were both virgins, but since I'd gained her trust, she let me convince her it would be okay, and we had sexual intercourse. When it was over, nothing was ever the same. In fact, as soon as I made the decision to do it, my soul felt as if a bomb had gone off and a war had erupted inside me. However, by then I couldn't stop. And worse, afterward, she naturally expected that she was my girlfriend, but I couldn't face her again."

Elliot's eyes were filled with pain. "Pastor Jack, I have gone before the Lord so many times. This happened six years ago. Even though I know that God has forgiven me for the horrible damage I did to that young woman and for compromising my own purity, I still can't shake this sense of condemnation in my soul.

"After graduation, I tried to find her to apologize and to ask for her forgiveness, but she seemed to have just vanished. Though I never again allowed myself to fall in that way, I am still, to this day, so burdened over it. Every time I set foot in the pulpit, every time I look into the faces of those broken people to whom God has sent me to minister deliverance and salvation, I feel crippled as an advocate for spiritual life and living—an actor playing the part of a preacher. It's worse than simply being terrified that I might be exposed as a moral fraud. It's feeling that I actually *am* one. I know it's ridiculous, but I can't get the idea out of my head. I know Christ has forgiven me, but a picture of the woman I violated seems to remain in my mind like an accusing finger pointing at me. That's why I wanted to see you. I have been seriously questioning whether I deserve to be in public ministry."

THWARTED BY THE ENEMY OF OUR SOULS

It's a syndrome from which many Christians suffer—a virus of guilt that won't go away. More than any other kind of sin, sexual sin produces guilt that cripples a believer's confidence and authority. Out of all the issues that people have brought to me, I've never had anyone say, "Pastor Jack, I just can't shake the feelings of guilt and condemnation I have from the time when I used to swear" or ". . . because I used to be a shoplifter" or ". . . because I used to really hate my Uncle Clyde."

But I cannot begin to tell you the number of times I have dealt with people who,

> though they walk with Christ,
> though they have been forgiven of their sins and the welter of other failures that may have characterized their lives,
> though they have no question that the Word of God says they have been forgiven,
> though their transgressions have been made as far as the east is from the west,

they remain still bound by a crippling sense of condemnation because of sexual sin.

It is out of the decades-long parade of brokenness and damage that have crossed my door as a pastor that I am so impassioned about the fact that sex sins are *not* the same as other sins—that they are, in fact, worse. I weary of watching the crippling imprint of guilt and condemnation linger in too many believers, long after they have confessed and repented and have been granted God's release to be free from all shame and guilt.

Generally speaking, this sense of guilt and shame does not persist because the individuals do not understand God's forgiveness; it persists because of two dynamics: first, the brutality of the adversary, and second, the vulnerability of our sexuality to unique psychological wounding. The Bible says that Satan is the "accuser of our brethren" (Rev. 12:10). He is *relentless*—accusing us day and night in spite of God's grace and goodness. Further, when people surrender to sexual sin, it is common for something real to become lodged in their souls—something fixes itself in the psyche, like a monument to their failure.

Many believers, like Elliot, though they have turned away from that sin and have never gone back, experience a lurking sense of condemnation that may taunt and haunt them for *years*, impeding any confidence that entrance into a fully untainted, freed and dynamic life in Christ can ever be truly known. Relationships are often dulled or neutralized. Movement forward into the service to which God has called them—as an overflowing avenue of His grace and life to others—is halted.

In contrast, God's Word declares it is the destiny of *everyone* whose life has been redeemed by the blood of Jesus Christ to be as "kings and priests" (Rev. 1:6)—certified and authorized instruments of God's glory and goodness, ministering to others His dominion here on Earth. That's a promise and potential for more than just Christian leaders who train for pastoral ministry. It's for you, dear one in Christ. People like *you*—the bus driver, soccer mom, office worker, schoolteacher, doctor, computer repair technician or supermarket clerk. Your mission field is your family, your workplace, the town in which you live, your neighbors and the people you meet every day. Kingdom life—the life of Christ's kingdom of priests and kings—is the fruit of faithful discipleship through each one of us who names the name of Jesus. But nothing seems to thwart that discipleship as effectively as the hammering lies of the enemy—a "ministry" that *he* tirelessly renders to bring guilt and condemnation to our souls and to intimidate us from pursuing emboldened, Spirit-filled ministry.

ROBBED OF THE JOY OF OUR SALVATION

Do you not know that the unrighteous will not inherit the kingdom of God? Do not be deceived. Neither fornicators, nor idolaters, nor adulterers, nor homosexuals, nor sodomites, nor thieves, nor covetous, nor drunkards, nor revilers, nor extortioners will inherit the kingdom of God. And such were some of you.

1 CORINTHIANS 6:9-11

The apostle Paul, in writing here about the "unrighteous," is addressing a body of believers living in a city known for its gross sexual immorality. He lists a catalog of sins characterizing sexual impurity and says that those who commit them will be disinherited from the Kingdom. Does that mean that people who engage in sexual sin will lose their salvation? No. Rather, what the Word of God is saying is that sex sins obliterate the confidence, authority, power and blessings of the Kingdom—as they did in Elliot's life. Sex sins tend to dull our souls to the God-given joy of our salvation, robbing us of the strength that joy is designed to sustain (see Neh. 8:9-12).

Elliot was not the first person to find himself still stricken long after his failure and his subsequent repentance. One full year after falling into grotesque sexual sin with Bathsheba, David appealed to the Lord as one in a *covenant* relationship with God—in other words, as one who is saved. He says, "Restore to me the joy of Your salvation" (Ps. 51:12). These are the words of a man who knew God's heart as well as anyone and yet still carried the shame and pain of his failure. Who can argue that sex sins aren't fiercely damaging when a man as mighty and understanding of the heart of God as David, one year after he had sinned, was still struggling with guilt and shame?

"Blot out my transgressions," was David's plea. "Wash me thoroughly from my iniquity, and cleanse me from my sin. For I acknowledge my transgressions, and my sin is always before me. Create in me a clean heart" (Ps. 51:1-3,10). No person whose heart is totally given over to the Lord is ever ineligible for such renewal and revival. David's testimony reminds us, however, that even if we don't lose our relationship with God, if as believers we have even an *instance* of failure in our sexual purity, we may lose our confidence of peace and authority in our Kingdom lives.

> Who can argue that sex sins aren't fiercely damaging when a man as mighty and understanding of the heart of God as David, one year after he had sinned, was still struggling with guilt and shame?

Be very clear, however, that I am not describing people who *persist* in sexual sin. To walk that path breeds more than condemnation. Such casual or presumptuous behavior is different from what we've discussed here, and sensed guilt in such cases is not an accusation of the adversary but a warning from the Spirit of God who is *convicting*, not condemning. The Holy Spirit is calling sinners to repentance, not to mere remorse.

REDEEMED IN FULL

Now, however, look at the *hope* God offers to any of us who have failed and felt the misery. A catalog of sinning that's as distressing as any you could imagine was outlined to the believers at Corinth by the apostle Paul: fornication, idolatry, adultery, homosexuality, sodomy, thievery, covetousness, drunkenness, slander and extortion (see 1 Cor. 6:9-10). Paul had been their pastor in the past and "knew them when." But later, to assure them of Christ's perfect and full grace to the formerly fallen, he follows that horribly grotesque list with these words: "And such were some of you. But you were washed, but you were sanctified, but you were justified in the name of the Lord Jesus and by the Spirit of our God" (v. 11).

That's the good news I gave Elliot—and it's for every sincere believer like him who may be trapped in past memories. Hear it, dear fellow servant: You are not disqualified! Jesus has guaranteed you full forgiveness and has granted you full authority as His representative to your world. Stand up! Look up! And be who He's made and redeemed you to be and to become.

Elliot had asked me, "Pastor Jack, what if it's too late? What good can I do now?" The answer: *It's never too late.* That's the whole message of the gospel. Christ's saving work on the cross has established our complete redemption. He has bought back everything that was lost, He has met and mastered the enemy, and now He calls us to apply that victory in our lives. No matter how polluted the past, *now* we are washed, sanctified and justified in the name of our Lord Jesus by the Spirit of God.

Today, Elliot is serving faithfully and fruitfully in the Kingdom authority that is his through Jesus Christ. So can any of us who are His. But anyone who tries to suggest that sex sins don't produce a more caustic and tenacious dimension of guilt in believers than that caused by other sins isn't being honest about this human response to the massive violations that sex sins cause. Even so, there's a "Hallelujah!" waiting for those of us who receive the freeing truth of God's Word. Read it—then shout that word of triumph!

HELP UNTO HOPE AND HEALING

*Walk in the Spirit, and you shall not fulfill the lust of the flesh. Those
who practice such things will not inherit the kingdom of God. But
the fruit of the Spirit is love, joy, peace, longsuffering, kindness, goodness,
faithfulness, gentleness, self-control. . . . And those who are Christ's
have crucified the flesh with its passions and desires. If we live in the
Spirit, let us also walk in the Spirit.*
GALATIANS 5:16,21-25

*There is therefore now no condemnation to those who are in Christ
Jesus, who do not walk according to the flesh, but according to the Spirit.*
ROMANS 8:1

Examining Myself

Where in my life have I given ground to the enemy of my soul to
taunt me with accusations and condemnation? Have I whole-
heartedly repented and applied the redeeming blood of Jesus
to that situation? What memories need to be brought to the
feet of Jesus, rather than be run and rerun on the screen of my
mind?

Turning to the Lord in Prayer

*Lord, in Jesus' name, I renounce every tie and bond to any
person or habit of sexual sin that may continue to snag me and
interfere with my growth and maturity as Your servant.
I thank You, Lord God, for the revealing, delivering and healing grace that You are filling me with now in those wounded
places where Satan would like to continue to keep me
ensnared. I receive Your liberty and declare Your victory in my
mind, body, spirit and soul from this day forward. Amen.*

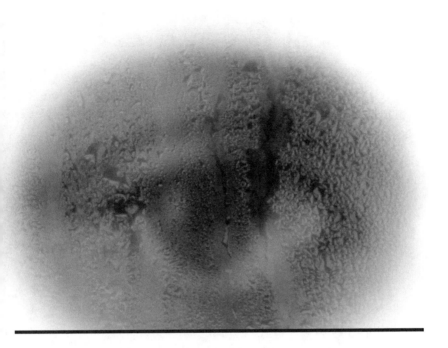

CHAPTER SIX

SEX SINS COMPROMISE THE FOUNDATION OF LIFE'S DEEPEST RELATIONSHIP — MARRIAGE

Husbands, love your wives, just as Christ also loved the church and gave Himself for her. Wives, submit to your own husbands, as to the Lord.

EPHESIANS 5:25,22

The perforation that takes place in a life that has been eroded through sexual sins sorely undermines the foundational strength of those footings that are intended to contribute to a joyous future. Sexual integrity between men and women at a personal and intimate level is an essential element for building toward fulfillment. So examine with me now the fifth reason why sex sins are worse than others: Sex sins compromise the foundation of life's deepest human relationship—marriage.

It was as if a dark cloud came in the door with Lily and Cooper when they walked into my office. They could barely speak to one another. Guilt, resentment and frustration were lurking behind their silence.

It had been three months since Cooper had confessed to a sexual encounter with a woman he'd met while out of town on business. Cooper said that since his and Lily's baby had been born nearly a year before, Lily had paid less attention to him, and he'd been unfaithful because he felt like his wife didn't care for him. After he had confessed and repented, Lily said that she forgave him, but deep inside her heart, she was still wounded and unhealed, holding on to residual anger and resentment. Though her pain was fully understandable, her unforgiveness maintained the barricade that Cooper had erected by his unfaithfulness.

They hadn't communicated well or resumed their sexual relationship since then. Though they loved one another enough to seek help, their lives were clearly flowing in opposite directions. "It's not that I don't forgive him," said Lily, "but I just can't get it out of my mind that he was with another woman, especially after we had our baby. Every time he starts to touch me, I think about him with her. I just can't go through with it; I still hurt so much."

Now, deeply ashamed at how his sin of adultery had caused such devastating damage, Cooper made further admissions to Lily, because their private conversations had deepened his sense of responsibility and pressed him to confess: He had also become driven to pornography and masturbation, practices he had only dabbled in earlier in their marriage but which he now attempted to rationalize by reason of Lily's withdrawal.

Lily and Cooper's is not an unusual case of major damage—the injuries caused by sex sins merge synergistically into full-blown assault on marital union. Marriage is life's deepest, most precious and potentially most fulfilling human relationship. Indeed, its depth is demonstrated in the fact that throughout the Bible marriage is used to describe our relationship with Jesus Christ as His redeemed—His Bride.

In 2 Corinthians 11:2, the apostle Paul uses the tenderness and purity inherent in the marriage relationship to express to the church at Corinth his desire for its fidelity to the Savior: "For I have betrothed you to one husband, that I may present you as a chaste virgin to Christ." Thus, it is in the spiritual union of Jesus with His Bride, the Church, that we see modeled the intended order for the partnering of men and women so that the rich fulfillment God intended for marriage may be realized and preserved.

THE ONE FLESH OF MARRIAGE

He who made them at the beginning "made them male and female,"
and said, "For this reason a man shall leave his father and mother and
be joined to his wife, and the two shall become one flesh" . . . Therefore
what God has joined together, let not man separate.

MATTHEW 19:4-6

When we enter into marriage, it is important to first realize how the collective damage caused by earlier sexual sin can inhibit success from the start. If either partner's identity, emotionality, creativity or spiritual authority has been compromised—issues we've already discussed—those compromises are almost certain to become a potential time bomb. When infused into a marriage, hidden or undealt with sex sins are only too ready to later implode this most fundamental of all human relationships. Believers who have engaged in sex sins prior to their marriage—or who have been damaged by the negative modeling of a parent—bring the uninvited, corrosive elements of guilt, shame and fear into marriage. Unless these issues are worked through with the help of premarital counsel or addressed through candid transparency with one another in private, they inevitably reduce the prospect of healthy, open communication that is essential in order for this highest of all human relationships to prosper.

The sexual relationship within marriage is infinitely more than merely a physical activity. It is a *self-disclosure*. And if hidden shame or guilt has not been removed, the end result will either be a distancing from one another or the reduction of sexual interaction to the plane of mere pleasure. While the pleasurable joys of marriage's sexual union are certainly appropriate and God-intended, they only remain so when we give ourselves wholly to one another. Hidden guilt, secret sin, compromise via flirtation, private thoughts and the plethora of visualizations that pornography introduces into the psyche—all cheapen the preciousness of the sexual relationship and undermine its durability as a truly intimate sharing of souls as well as bodies.

The sheer forces of relativism, humanism and hedonism in our culture have eroded foundational views long held sacred and have brought with them a devastating amount of scarring that prevents genuine sexual fulfillment within marriage for many people. The Bible reveals that sexual relations, as designed by God within the context of marriage, are for (1) procreation (see Gen. 1:22), (2) expression of unity (see Gen. 2:24), (3) expression of affection and comfort (see Gen. 24:67; Song of Sol. 2:10), and (4) mutual enjoyment (see Prov. 5:18). How tragically those things are lost when sexual sin compromises a marriage.

Satan is hell-bent on attacking our sexuality, because our sexuality not only expresses our deepest union but also is the source of our highest physical satisfaction. Forgive me for stating it so bluntly: Orgasms were invented by God. That He created this staggeringly marvelous capacity for fulfillment should tell us something about God's intentions toward us. If you need further evidence that, at a physical level, the marriage relationship is not so "spiritual" as to be improper, I invite you to read the Song of Solomon, an open and joyous declaration of this awesome gift to God's people.

Yet when it comes to our sexuality, the world's covetous attitude that "more is better" ("more" being perverted or polluted pursuits) is diametrically opposed to the highest fulfillment God intends for our lives. When the Lord gives the restriction that our sexual activity ought to be confined to one person for a lifetime within the context of marriage, it isn't because He's trying to keep us from having the most fun. On the contrary: God has designed for us maximum enjoyment, and His Word provides those restrictions and guidelines intended to advance and preserve that enjoyment.

SATISFACTION IN RELATIONSHIP, NOT JUST IN BODIES

I'll call him Jim—a really good guy and solid Christian. He and his wife, Amy, were a strong part of our church family. But as he sat in my office, I sensed his awkward feelings about the subject he was about to introduce. "Jim, you asked to have a little time together, and I want to thank you for coming to talk. But hey," I laughed, "you seem about as nervous as the hot-tin-roof cat!" His laughter relaxed his tension, as I hoped it would, and he got right to the point.

"Pastor Jack, I guess any guy feels awkward, especially being as young as I am—still in my 30s—and I'm wrestling with being unable to pursue Amy's and my sex life *at all*. I've become absolutely disabled in the bedroom." He chuckled again, but it was the laugh of embarrassment, not humor.

Without rehearsing the whole conversation, what surfaced was so simple a fact that Jim was amazed it had made so great a difference in the intimate details of his marriage. When I inquired—actually asking the question I did by the prompting of the Holy Spirit—I found that he and Amy had been attempting to make love only and always with all the lights out in their bedroom.

Needless to say, the darkness itself wasn't a particular problem, but as we talked, Jim recognized how much the absence of eye-to-eye contact while making love had removed the richness of true person-to-person communication from his and Amy's sexual relationship. What might have at first seemed romantic (and for a given situation or situations, could well be) had unwittingly caused their sexual interaction to become merely physical. Not long after our talk, Jim confided in me that a return to soft lighting (and even a little romantic music) had brought back the communication that restored the depth of desire and vitality that both of them longed for.

Jim and Amy's experience didn't involve sexual sin, unless sin is described as missing the intended goal, which in the case of sexual intimacy is the nurturing of love's bonds and the deepening of interpersonal communication. Their case points to the wild procession of thought and attitude in our present culture that regards the sexual act as a *goal*—the reduction of life to the merely physical realm, often to the violation of the psychological and spiritual health of persons.

Let me reinforce a gargantuan fact that our present culture will never suggest to you, because it has never learned it: Genuine sexual fulfillment is found in the *relationship* between people, not merely in the mechanics of their bodies. A couple's sexual relationship is not simply a *part* of their relationship; its intimacy, its act of complete openness, its mutual surrender and its self-giving comprise the very *definition* of marriage's intent.

> A couple's sexual relationship is not simply a *part* of their relationship; its intimacy, its act of complete openness, its mutual surrender and its self-giving comprise the very *definition* of marriage's intent.

Marriage contains a multitude of components—especially as a couple's life together develops on several fronts. Marriage's domestic details, the arrival of children, the management of finances, relationships with in-laws, spiritual growth and service to and for the Lord—these and a host of other things are all *part*. But after counseling multiplied thousands of people during my years of pastoral ministry, I've found that the most revealing place to begin unraveling the tangle of marital problems is to ask a couple about their sexual relationship. This is not born of any preoccupation or belief I have in Freudian psychological theorems and certainly not because the subject is titillating to one's curiosity. Asking a couple about their sexual relationship is simply the most direct route to finding out if the couple's life together is being nourished by openness, honesty, unselfishness in giving themselves to their union and maintained in an atmosphere of forthrightness. Sexual union—pure and simple—addresses all these issues. (As an aside, let me simply note that this fact is the reason that all other sexual investments—adultery, pornography, masturbation, flirtation and the exploration of bizarre behaviors—*never, never durably satisfy.*)

Precisely because the sexual aspect of a couple's relationship is the focal point of their marriage, the adversary hammers at it the most intensely. Sexual sin splinters unity between a husband and wife, breaches fidelity and trust, and corrodes the expansion of their intimacy. It poisons the possibility of the most open, sensitive and precious communication between husband and wife, and annuls, for many, the unique blessing that comes from having been with only one person sexually for a lifetime.

PURITY RESTORED

Before we were married, Anna and I were college kids, as fired with the heat of young passion as any couple. But we weren't simply ignited by sexual desire—we genuinely loved and cared about each other. We had grown in our relationship to a place of commitment to be married, so we got engaged. As we counted the months until our wedding, saving ourselves until marriage was not without a struggle. There was a fully explainable, entirely human, not inappropriate, fiery, natural desire in us to be together sexually.

Now, what I am about to say is not intended to inflict guilt on any reader or to bring a reminder of failure to anyone; but Anna and I were both raised to believe that we ought to remain virgins until we were married, and when we joined together on our wedding night, we did, indeed, arrive there as such.

I relate that victory to highlight the reward we received for our having persevered through the struggle to overcome temptation: Standing on the horizon of our fiftieth wedding anniversary, my dear wife and I have the joyous testimony that, in our lifetime, we have *both* the fulfilling sense of only belonging to one another and the inexplicable delight found in God's way for human sexual union. Our chastity and our fidelity do not mean that we were neither tempted before our marriage nor untested by temptation during it. Rather, they are results born of a commitment to the truth and promise of God's Word, and fulfillment brought about by the power of the Holy Spirit's working Christ's life in two mere humans who have been open to His ability to bring strength in the midst of our weakness and joy through our simple obedience. Our success in remaining pure encourages me to believe that any believer can *if Jesus is asked into the equation and the spirit of this world is refused its cheap offer.*

If you will never have the testimony that Anna and I have, you are not disqualified from the fulfillment of sexual purity in marriage. I believe that among the things the Lord would like to do in the Church today, by the work of His Holy Spirit, is to raise up a redeemed generation out of the rubble of sexual sin—people who know what it means to be restored to purity, to be, as Paul wrote to the Corinthians, presented as chaste virgins to Christ (see 2 Cor. 11:2).

That promise of being presented to Christ as a chaste virgin is still possible for you, even if you have failed, because Jesus came to redeem and restore, to forgive and recover. Our reminder of the destructiveness of sex sins—our study of their devastation—is not to remove hope for true fulfillment any more than it is to argue against God's great forgiveness. But what has been compromised needs to be *confessed* so that what has been broken will be *restored*.

Open your heart to God's grace and power. And if you are married or moving toward marriage, open your hearts to one another. Receive godly counsel that can deliver, and open yourselves to receiving the deliverance that paves the way to God's fulfillment in your marriage.

Anna and I are more than ready to assure you: It isn't too late.

HELP UNTO HOPE AND HEALING

Let each one of you in particular so love his own wife as himself, and let the wife see that she respects her husband.

EPHESIANS 5:33

Examining Myself

Where have I compromised the trust, fidelity and sacredness of my marriage? In what areas have I avoided communicating with my spouse?

Turning to the Lord in Prayer

Lord, I confess my sins to You now and ask You to deliver me from habits that compromise or threaten my marriage. I cast down every vain imagination that has caused me to think of myself as independent from the "one flesh" that You've declared over me and my spouse. Show me how to be both forgiving and forgiven, and restore my marriage to the purity that brings profound happiness and glorifies You. In Jesus' name, I pray, amen.

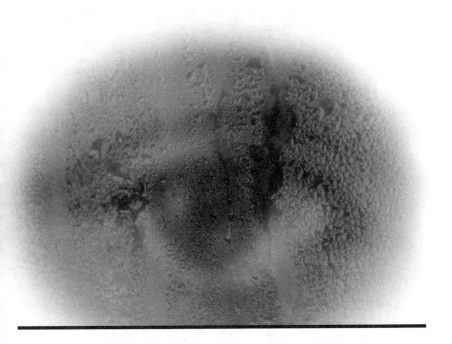

CHAPTER SEVEN

SEX SINS EXPOSE US TO THE RISK OF BEGETTING AN UNSUPPORTED HUMAN BEING

When my father and my mother forsake me, then the LORD will take care of me.

PSALM 27:10

The sixth reason why sex sins are worse than others is because they expose us to the risk of begetting an unsupported human being. Here the collateral damage of sexual immorality expands onto the destiny of others.

She was 16 years old. She was pregnant. And she was scared.

It was 1966, and even if abortion had been legally available, Melanie told me she wouldn't have had one. She said she'd felt an inexplicable and loving bond to the child growing inside her body. Terrified by what she anticipated would happen when her mother and father found out, she tried as long as she could to keep her pregnancy a secret from them. Her angry, brokenhearted and ashamed parents sent Melanie to another town to have the baby in secret. She lived for six months under an assumed name at a home for unwed mothers, while her parents told relatives that Melanie was away at private school. When her baby was born, Melanie was given no option but to relinquish the infant for adoption. Told to go home and pretend it never happened, Melanie was never allowed to talk openly about her sexual activity as an unmarried teenager, or about her firstborn child, whom she'd given away. Until their deaths some 20 years later, Melanie's parents never acknowledged their grandchild.

In today's world, this scenario (with its secrecy and shame, struggles and pain) does not have to occur, because, as wrong as it is, any teenage girl, sometimes even without the permission of her parents, can opt for an abortion, can casually dispense with a life, with great privacy, ease and social approval. In saying this, I certainly do not mean to trivialize the emotional shock and family stress that teen pregnancy introduces. But integrity with regard to the larger issues of our humanity, the value of life itself and the realities inherent in the known impact of abortion demand that we deal *first* with the question: Does ending the life of an unborn child bring any *less* suffering?

The answer is proven—verified by millions who, in the aftermath of an abortion, carry scars at multiple dimensions. The tally of long-term emotional, spiritual (and sometimes physical) damage to those who have participated in abortion reveals the gruesome truth: There is no painless way out of the consequences of sexual sin.

Does ending the life of an unborn child bring any *less* suffering?

Though she struggled with how it was going to change her life, Melanie somehow knew in her heart that the miracle of creation was taking place inside of her body. Even her worst fears about being pregnant couldn't convince her that killing that life would annul it. Notwithstanding her violation of God's Word, Melanie had not yet become calloused, and she later testified to an inner consciousness of the fact she had crossed a line—a line drawn by the creator's hand.

"I didn't know this Scripture at the time," Melanie told me, "but the reality of its implications registered at the moral center of my soul: 'For You [Lord] formed my inward parts; You covered me in my mother's womb'" (Ps. 139:13).

A CULTURE OF DEATH

Exposed as we are to more than three decades of the grinding social, cultural and legal pressure of *Roe Versus Wade*, young hearts in today's world so easily become calloused to the preciousness and deep purposes of our sexual capacity, as well as to the sanctity of human life. By the time they reach Melanie's age, millions of young hearts have already been hardened by the death-dealing decision of our United States Supreme Court (a decision which, years ago, was renounced by the case's lead plaintiff herself). Women and men, deceived into believing that they have been "liberated" from the consequences of unwanted pregnancy as a result of sexual sin, pursue with relative abandon a path that not only destroys the life taken by abortion but also works destruction in the souls of those who take that course.

Though people assume that by choosing abortion they will become free of the consequences of unwanted pregnancy, the indelible imprint of the creator's love-gift of a life that once was present in the womb results in an inescapably abiding consciousness. Just as Melanie said to me, so the same words have been admitted over and over again by those honest enough to confess them: "I wasn't ever able to pretend it never happened."

Melanie's ever-raw wound of having given birth to a baby to whom she could not be a mother went unattended for decades. She told me her heart ached every time she saw a mom pushing her infant in a stroller. As well, a peculiar wall entered her and her parents' intercommunication, a kind of polite truce—an unnaturalness that, while it did not block a continued relationship, still obstructed any dimension of meaningful communication they may have had before "the event." That wall persisted through the balance of their years, and the interaction that could have led to forgiveness and restoration was never realized. Hypnotized by the philosophy of a culture of denial and death, their act of dispensing of a life so cavalierly (without, at the time, grasping the implications of the decision they would make) erected a gravestone, like a punctuation mark, to their communication.

Despite society's sales pitch to the contrary, women and men who have chosen abortion will testify that they cannot pretend it never happened either. The same kind of woundedness and shame brings them to the offices of pastors like myself too often—bleeding emotionally, tormented by guilt and hoping to find counsel that may lead to their deliverance. Their loss is tragically deeper than they were ever given to suppose, for they never imagined that a literal death would actually be occurring at their own hands.

The Meaning of "Unsupported"

Abortion is not the only way a life conceived in sexual sin can be unsupported. Indeed, not every child aborted by a parent or parents was necessarily conceived out of wedlock. Today, abortion is regularly practiced by married people, so neither fornication nor adultery was involved. Neither infidelity nor irresponsibility was the cause of the pregnancy; only the attitude that is manifest in failing to steward the life that was conceived was.

When I say "unsupported," I am referring to two additional general categories, besides the child who is unsupported *in the womb*—whose life has been ended by abortion. The first is a child who is given life but who is unsupported by any of the many ways that a child may be *abandoned* by one or both parents. This includes such cases as the newborn left to die in a trash can and discovered by a passerby; the toddler who is bounced around foster homes; the teen whose father or mother either was never present or deserted the family. And the beat goes on.

Second, a child may be unsupported *emotionally*—told that he or she was a mistake and treated as unwanted, unworthy and undesirable. The words may never be spoken, but the echoes continue interminably in the mind of a child who believes that he or she was never meant to be born. Often a sense of futility and awkwardness accompanies the child's thoughts of his or her birth. By such a lack of support, innumerable people have suffered the contamination of so many aspects of their developing sense of personhood, the shaping of their personality and the formation of their subsequent relationships.

Some years ago, one of the most devoted Christians I've ever known shared with me the distressing discovery that he had been conceived out of wedlock and that his parents had gotten married only out of obligation because his mother was pregnant. This discovery sent him into an emotional upheaval. This mature believer in Christ suddenly felt a sense of not having been wanted—that the very origin of his life was without the support of his parents.

Another young man I know told me that when his parents died, he found among their papers a document revealing that he had been adopted—a significant fact that he'd never been told. Ever since childhood, Dave could remember having unresolved feelings about himself, but his parents brushed them off as adolescent awkwardness. Finding the adoption agency's documents detailing that his birth mother had signed away her rights to keep him and those signed by his parents applying to adopt a child who had not yet been named filled Dave with humiliation and a profound sense of rejection and pain. Not only had his birth mother not wanted him, but also, Dave reasoned, if his parents couldn't reveal to him who he really was, they must have been ashamed of him, too. (I want to distinguish Dave's story from the very loving and often lovely stories of those children who have been given up for adoption by loving mothers, but whose situations were such that they believed adoption to be the better course. In my view, this is not a case of "unsupport"; rather, such action reflects one of the ways that the biblical *spiritual* principle of adoption becomes a *redemptive* principle in caring for a human life.)

Love and Acceptance from Father God

*Nevertheless the solid foundation of God stands, having this
seal: "The Lord knows those who are His."*
2 TIMOTHY 2:19

I've often found that people who grew up as unsupported children have a difficult time understanding and receiving the love
of Father God. Children who are physically or emotionally
abandoned by their earthly parents have, however unwittingly,
been introduced to a false "theology" of God. Many parents
have little comprehension of the profound fact that, at least
until children are five to seven years old, *parents are the essential
theological textbook instructing children in the character, constancy and
concern of God Himself.* Unsupported children move into life
with little on which to base their sense of what God may be
like; their view of the original life-giver is distorted by the ways
of the human beings who were His instruments in giving them
life. Thus, their trust in a heavenly Father can be eroded or distorted for their entire lives. Without parental wisdom, love,
care and acceptance, children whose origin is in sexual sin will
too often be more vulnerable to those things that lead to
disorder, deteriorative habits and, in time, deep spiritual and
physical bondage.

No unsupported child needs to live in condemnation and
shame. The great prophetic message of the Lord is His promise
to lift us up if our mother or father forsakes us (see Ps. 27:10). As
with the damage caused by *all* sin, there is healing, recovery and
restoration available through Jesus, our redeemer, to any person
who began life as an unsupported human being. God does not
have a tentative attitude toward any of His children. He is not

uncertain about whether or not He loves us. His Word declares that His thoughts toward us are of "peace and not of evil, to give you a future and a hope" (Jer. 29:11). Indeed, the message of the gospel is based on God's love for us: "For God so loved the world that He gave His only begotten Son, that whoever believes in Him should not perish but have everlasting life" (John 3:16).

One of the most profound testimonies that I have ever been privileged to hear was that of a young woman named Gianna, whom I invited several years ago to minister at our church. Gianna's mother had attempted to abort Gianna in the womb. By the grace of God, Gianna was born anyway, and though severely disabled from the trauma of the attempted abortion, her loveliness, intelligence and singing voice had not been impaired. She radiated the beauty and victory of Jesus Christ and sensed she had been divinely called to minister to others. Satan's hateful attempt to cut off Gianna's life backfired into a mission that has since blessed a large number of other wounded people.

LOVE AND ACCEPTANCE FROM EARTHLY PARENTS

In contrast to the brokenness that attends unsupported children, what a joy for a couple to be able to say to their kids, "You were born out of the love between your mother and father. We were so happy when we knew you were coming!" They may not even have planned their children according to a schedule, but because they value life intrinsically and their children personally, they are able to say, "*We wanted you,* and we're so glad you were born!"

That is the testimony of our family. Anna and I have four children: Two were born by the chart—at exactly the time we planned. The next two had nothing to do with a chart—they simply arrived and our youngest child was a complete surprise. (I've always felt that the Lord did that just to show us that we weren't so smart after all!)

Anna and I were married three years before we started our family, and then our first three children were born in the next five years. Our plan was to stop there, but years later we had the surprise of a new arrival. Needless to say, we welcomed this prospect, but it became a lesson to us in the difference between God's sovereign purposes and human planning. I often encourage couples facing the similar "inconvenience" of an unexpected child because of our discovery of the blessing and *purpose* in God's timing of our youngest. Her arrival into our family became not only a profound joy to us but also a wonderful instrument of instruction enabling us to minister to even more families, since ours spanned nearly a generation.

CONFUSION IN THE COURT AND IN THE COMMUNITY

Monumental confusion also takes place in a society in which abortion flourishes. As the law stands today, a mother who, by reason of her ingestion of narcotics, *accidentally* kills her unborn child can be prosecuted for murder.[1] So, too, can a person whose actions inadvertently cause the death of a pregnant woman's fetus. However, the mother who *intentionally* kills her unborn child by means of abortion has committed no crime.

Spreading this madness to the Christian community are those who are guided by confusion and compelled by some distorted sense of moral obligation to blow up abortion clinics or to injure or kill people in the name of life. Recently, a horribly tragic case involved a former Presbyterian minister—holding fast to his claim that he'd acted on behalf of saving lives—who became the first person executed for having murdered an abortion doctor. His supporters called him a martyr.[2] No matter what we may think about the wrongness of abortion, the murder of its proponents is an instigation of the enemy at his deceptive worst.

AN INCALCULABLE LOSS

Can we begin to imagine how different our world would be today if the multiplied millions of lives who have been aborted had been allowed to live? As stated earlier, more than *43 million* human beings have been legally aborted *in the United States alone.*[3] This isn't even counting the vast numbers in other countries. With each case of moral failure, sex sins compound unto a loss that impacts the *entire world.* What difference could one life make? If, as the environmentalist legitimately argues, the extinction of a single species of bird or bug can alter the ecology of an entire region of our planet, how much more significant is a human life—*one that might have found a cure for cancer, one that might have negotiated a peace, one that might have led thousands to Christ and to eternal salvation?* How many great thinkers and achievers of our time have been *lost to us forever* among the millions of lives cut off in the womb?

There is no question about it: Sex sins are worse than others in many regards, but possibly none more dramatic than in the way they so often beget unsupported human beings—or short-circuited ones, who are conceived but never allowed a chance to be.

Again, dear one, if any of this chapter indicts you at a tragic point of your past, know this: Sex sins are not harder for God to forgive—not even the sin of abortion. The Bible declares, "God demonstrates His own love toward us, in that while we were still sinners, Christ died for us" (Rom. 5:8). Further, if you or someone you know began life as an unsupported human being, or if your heart was broken over the aborting, abandoning or forsaking of a child, please accept the invitation to enter the loving, accepting, redeeming presence of Father God through His Son, Jesus Christ. In His presence, we are always assured to find His releasing forgiveness and the entrance to peace and new purpose in life.

HELP UNTO HOPE AND HEALING

The Spirit of the LORD is upon Me, because He has . . .
sent Me to heal the brokenhearted.
LUKE 4:18

Examining Myself
What does abortion, adoption or abandonment mean to me in my life? What does it mean to my ability to minister to others? Of whom does this chapter make me think? To whom may I minister healing, support and love?

Turning to the Lord in Prayer
If you began life as an unsupported human being, this prayer is for you.

Father God, Your Word declares that You set the solitary in families [see Ps. 68:6]. Thank You for adopting me into Your family through the sacrifice of Your Son, Jesus [see Gal. 4:4-6]. Thank You for being my heavenly Father, who created me in Your image and unto Your glory. I forgive my earthly mother

and father for their sins against me, and I release them
into Your recovery and restoration. Now, Lord, in the place
where I was unsupported, be my rock, my deliverer
and my foundation. As I release to You the hurt and
confusion I've felt about myself, I welcome an abundance
of Your life into every one of those empty places. You have
already declared that I am Your child in Christ.
Thank You, Lord, for there is none like You. Amen.

If you have sinned by begetting an unsupported being, this prayer is for you.

Father God, I thank You with all my heart that
You have provided the ultimate atonement for my sins in
the sacrifice of Your Son, Jesus. I bring to that cross of such
unimaginable suffering the suffering that I caused to
my child and the guilt, shame and suffering that I have felt
because of it. I dedicate my child to You, Lord—whether
he or she is living on Earth or in heaven—and I surrender
what remains of my life here on Earth to walk in sexual purity
and righteousness before You. Turn my mourning into
dancing, Lord [see Ps. 30:11], and just as You have redeemed
and restored my life, make me an instrument of Your grace
and redemption to others. In Jesus' name, amen.

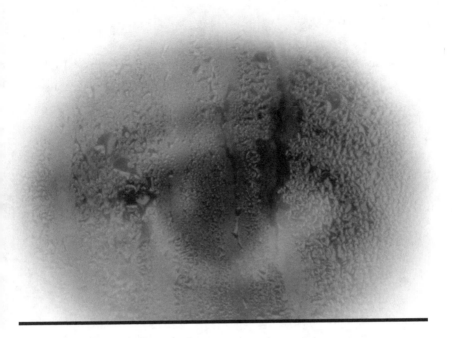

CHAPTER EIGHT

SEX SINS INCREASE THE PROBABILITY OF MULTIPLYING THE SPREAD OF DISEASE

If you diligently heed the voice of the LORD your God and do what is right in His sight, give ear to His commandments and keep all His statutes, I will put none of the diseases on you which I have brought on the Egyptians. For I am the LORD who heals you.

EXODUS 15:26

The seventh reason why sex sins are worse than others is because sex sins increase the probability of multiplying the spread of disease. With that, an unintended dynamic of death may also be set into motion. The following letter illustrates the tragic consequences of the spread of disease that can result from just one instance of sexual sin.

Dear Pastor Jack,

A one-night stand changed my life forever. I don't know why I let myself be seduced, but I did, by a guy I barely knew and never saw again. I was in my 20s, and I didn't pay much attention to the pain that I began to feel after we had been together. By the time I went to the doctor, the gonorrhea had infected my fallopian tubes. I was told I might have scar tissue, but once I took the medication and the pain went away, I didn't think about it again. I didn't want to. I was totally ashamed and felt like I'd gotten what I deserved for having been so stupid. I wondered how many other people had become infected by this same guy and then passed the disease along to someone else.

A few years later I met a wonderful, Christian man, and we got married. We both wanted a big family and were thrilled when I got pregnant. But about six weeks into my pregnancy, while at work, I doubled over in pain and was rushed to the hospital, where they had to perform emergency surgery. Because of the scar tissue on my fallopian tube, the embryo hadn't been able to pass through to my uterus and had gotten stuck. At six weeks, its size was big enough to burst the tube, and I nearly hemorrhaged to death. By the time they finally opened me up to operate, over half my blood was in my stomach, and the nurse told me later that had they waited 15 minutes longer before operating, I would have died.

I lost my right fallopian tube as well as our baby. The doctor who performed the surgery told me that my other tube was also badly scarred and was adamant that I should avoid becoming pregnant because of the high probability that the same thing might happen again. Next time, he told me, I might not be so "lucky."

Vanessa

Sex sin increases the probability of multiplying the spread of disease. How much do we need to say about that?

Evidently a lot.

Fourteen thousand people *every day* become infected with HIV.

THE TWENTIETH-CENTURY PLAGUE

The number of people worldwide infected with or dying of AIDS has reached *40 million*.[1] And that number is *rising*. Fourteen thousand people *every day* become infected with HIV, the virus that causes AIDS, giving it the infamous title "twentieth century plague."[2] And more than half a million Americans have died from AIDS.[3] The United Nations estimates that nearly 70 million people will perish from AIDS-related diseases in the next two decades, and it's been said that "the worst is yet to come."[4]

The collateral damage inflicted by this sexually transmitted disease is equally staggering: It's predicted that more than 25 million youths will have lost at least one of their parents to AIDS by 2010—nearly double the number in 2003.[5] Think of the implications for our world of so many people orphaned, suffering and dying because of a sexually transmitted disease. Along with the profound loss of family that these children endure come malnutrition, abject poverty and the imprint of hopelessness. Where will the next generation of leaders come from in those nations ravaged by the AIDS epidemic?

With such clear evidence as to the devastating fatal outcome of this sexually transmitted disease, why are more and more people engaging in sexual behavior that invites infection? That question was posed to medical researchers in Britain who wrote: "Despite widespread awareness of HIV, the behavior of neither individuals nor governments has changed sufficiently to diminish the global pandemic." The researchers suggested that control of the epidemic was retarded by, among other things, "unwillingness to acknowledge risk" and "unwillingness to sacrifice sexual freedom."[6]

Ironically, those who have worked hard to mitigate the horrible suffering caused by AIDS have been indirectly responsible for its rise: With all the new medications available, many people are deluded into a false sense of security that AIDS no longer poses a deadly risk or that substantial resources are available to help them if they do get it. The blindness of the unregenerate human soul can be astounding.

The most tragic story I've been made aware of with regards to this issue has to do with girls in Uganda who were so committed to avoiding AIDS that they'd joined their school's Straight Talk Club, which promoted abstinence, a major theme of Uganda's anti-AIDS program. The story focused on Lillian, 16, who had been orphaned when both of her parents died of AIDS. Her uncle, who had been her guardian, also died of the disease, and Lillian, a leader in the Straight Talk Club, became more determined than ever to remain a virgin, finish school and go to college. But when her uncle died, there was no one left who could pay the $30 a month tuition for her schooling; and recently, some of the cousins with whom Lillian was living began to pressure her to raise money by finding a "sponsor"—that is, by selling her body. The abstinence clubs are popular in Uganda, the article said, but for many of the teenagers, sex is their only means of economic opportunity.[7]

THE NEW SCARLET LETTER

The crippling shame and emotional damage of sex sins leave a permanent mark on the psyche—and often a fatal mark in the flesh of a person who has contracted a sexually transmitted disease. The life of her child and her hope for a family had been devastated for Vanessa, the woman who wrote me that letter. Although accepted by her husband, forgiven by the Lord and now the adoptive parent of a child, Vanessa still struggled with the stain, shame and pain of a single act of sexual sin.

Since the AIDS epidemic, we haven't heard as much about the suffering that goes along with another incurable virus: herpes. But I have received innumerable letters from brokenhearted believers whose hopes and dreams for marriage have forever been altered because they know they will carry into that holy relationship the infection that resulted from sexual sin.

Should any believer in Jesus Christ think that the answer to this problem is in "safe" or "protected" sex with a condom, let me make it clear that there are no congratulations in order for this compromise. Not only is it a fact that condoms are not foolproof, the greater issue is that *there is no such thing as a casual Christian.*

I have met believers who actually thought that reducing the risk of pregnancy and disease by use of a condom justified their sexual immorality because they turned their immorality into a "Well, at least" issue. Dear ones, those who are redeemed in Jesus Christ are not intended to live life *at least*; they are intended to live life *at best*. Jesus tells us that He comes in order for us to have abundant life; it is Satan, the thief, who comes to reduce that prospect (see John 10:10). The distortion invited into the mind of believers who attempt to justify sexual sin is equivalent to opening one's door to robbers.

I was stunned by one believer who offered a popularized twist on Jesus' words. The person said to me, "Abundant life for me means freedom to indulge in sex on my own terms." How tragically confused! How sorely distorted! The standards set by the Word of God are not open to interpretation. God's conclusive directive on this issue distills into three words: *"Flee sexual immorality"* (1 Cor. 6:18, emphasis added).

As I have ministered extensively to wounded, hurting people, I have become aware that it's important that the Body of Christ not be loveless or exclusive in its attitude toward those who have become infected with sexually transmitted diseases, any more than Jesus rejected the leper. We are called to be agents of God's redemption not of His judgment. While sexual sins are more damaging than other sins—and in the case of AIDS, also isolating and fatal—they still are not harder for God to forgive. Neither does AIDS preclude any sincere believer's acceptance by God through Jesus Christ. All of us who have received Jesus Christ have been given an eternally healthy, sinless "blood transfusion." The blood of Christ not only redeems us by covering our sins but also purifies our souls by infusing us with the merits of Jesus' own purity. Regardless of the world's terminal prognosis, Jesus tells His disciples not to fear that which kills our bodies, but rather to fear (that is, to hold in reverence) "Him who is able to destroy both soul and body in hell" (Matt. 10:28).

God's promise to Israel in Exodus 15:26 holds true for us in our modern-day Egypt of unrestrained sexual indulgence: If we will heed His Word regarding sexual sin, we will not become subject to the death-dealing plague of its diseases. Just as the people of Israel stayed inside their homes with the blood of the Passover Lamb brushed onto their doorposts while death swept through the land, so we are all called to stay "under the blood" as we obediently abide by the terms of God's gracious protection.

Not only do sex sins increase the probability of multiplying the spread of disease to the body, but also they open the door for a virus to attack the soul—one that can ruin a lifetime's possibilities. And after all is said and done, even the world's "experts" have come to one conclusion: The key to avoiding venereal disease and AIDS is abstinence until marriage, and then, one partner for a lifetime. As one of my teenaged grandsons would mockingly say, "Like, *duh!* Who would have ever thought of that!"

HELP UNTO HOPE AND HEALING

Now a leper came to Him, imploring Him, kneeling down to Him and
saying to Him, "If You are willing, You can make me clean." Then
Jesus, moved with compassion, stretched out His hand and touched him,
and said to him, "I am willing; be cleansed."
MARK 1:40-41

Examining Myself
Have I ever tried to justify engaging in sexual sin? Has anyone I know ever been infected with a sexually transmitted disease? How has his or her life been affected as a result? Is there anyone

I know who is infected and needs my compassion, as he or she has now come to live repentantly in Christ?

Turning to the Lord in Prayer

Father God, in Jesus' name, I come before You now and seek Your light into every darkened area of my life. Where I have fallen prey to sexual sin and its damage, forgive me and heal me. Where I've stood in judgment of others, build in me compassion toward those who are hurting and sick because of sexual sin, and let me be an instrument of Your healing and redemption in their lives. Remove from me all fear of serving You alone, and deliver me from the self-righteousness that would cause me to draw back from the most wounded and suffering of Your children. Teach me how to love the leper, as Jesus did. Amen.

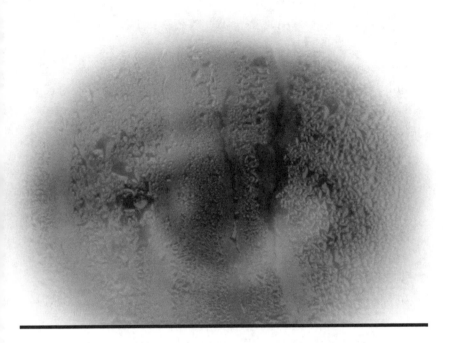

CHAPTER NINE

SEX SINS GIVE PLACE TO APPETITES THAT ONLY BEGET FURTHER IMMORAL BEHAVIOR

*Hell and Destruction are never full; so the
eyes of man are never satisfied.*

PROVERBS 27:20

It's the terrifying truth behind the seemingly harmless indul-
gences to which every one of us is exposed daily: Sex sins are

worse than other sins because they give place to appetites that only beget further immoral behavior. The following story of one young man's seduction is similar to that of so many who have fallen into the temptation trap.

Pete, age 19, had been over at a pal's house, watching the game and eating pizza with the guys. At halftime, his friend slipped a cassette into the VCR and suddenly Pete was confronted with the filth of a pornographic movie. All the other guys cheered. Too embarrassed to get up and walk out, Pete stayed in his seat and within a few minutes found himself captivated into not only watching but also identifying with the people on the screen and with the perverted things they were doing. Before long Pete was viewing sexually explicit movies and was buying pornographic magazines on a regular basis. Having given himself that license, it wasn't hard to begin rationalizing what came next.

"I didn't realize what I was being set up for," he told me. "All that watching . . . Eventually I had to start acting it out for myself. Masturbation didn't seem like such a bad thing to do; I mean, no one else got hurt or was put at risk or anything. But after a while that wasn't enough. I wanted to experience the thrills I saw those people having. At first I was scared that I was doing something wrong, but then that worry just seemed to go away. Once I'd started indulging, my passions took over, and I didn't care anymore. To be honest, it was exciting to be doing things that were so forbidden. After a few sexual encounters with girls I met through my friends, it became a regular part of my life to find opportunities for sex with all kinds of people—trying the things I saw the people doing in the magazines and videos.

"One day, I was at a coffee shop and I ran into this really nice Christian girl I had known in high school and had always liked. I used to tell myself that some day I was going to ask her out on date. But she was so pure and innocent, and when I looked at her, I felt like such trash. I really saw myself for the first time and could hardly believe what I'd done with my life. It made me sick."

What Pete didn't realize was that when he had opened himself up to looking at pornography, a *spiritual transaction* had taken place. His inheritance as a believer in Jesus Christ had been corrupted by a demon of lust.

DEMON SPIRIT BEHIND THE IMAGE

For this you know, that no fornicator, unclean person, nor covetous man, who is an idolater, has any inheritance in the kingdom of Christ and God.

EPHESIANS 5:5

Pete's indulgence in sexual sin may not have been a trade-off for his salvation, but it drastically contaminated his Kingdom inheritance of peace, joy, confidence and authority. Too many indulgent believers fail to realize the spiritual power behind pornographic images. What gave such compelling power to the images that Pete watched on the video, the *idol* he "worshiped" by looking at the magazines, was the *demon spirit* behind them. That's the definition of idolatry—*worshiping an image behind which a demon spirit resides.* By far, the most popular form of idolatry today is pornography. Your knee doesn't need to be literally bowed before it, but it's where you regularly come to "worship." In my years of pastoral counseling, I found pornography to be at the root of many people's problems related to sexual sin, especially for men. Sadly, however, increasing numbers of women are being lured by the same demonic attraction.

Sex sins give place to appetites that only beget further (and often increasingly degenerate) immoral behavior. The law of human flesh is that it is ruled by *covetousness*. The Greek word for covetousness, *pleonexia,* means a wanton quest that is insatiable and always seeking more. Expressed colloquially, it conveys the idea of an inordinate desire to have "what I want when I want it." The desire for a thing becomes the overwhelming drive in a person's soul—he or she can never get enough. The person becomes ensnared in the bondage of lust and turns the object of that lust's compulsion into an idol. So serious is the matter of covetousness that its prohibition is one of God's fundamental commandments (see Exod. 20:17). Pete, having given in to sexual indulgence, became swept up into an unappeasable habit that quickly turned into a powerful addiction.

People struggle with addictions of all kinds, which are often demonically resourced and administrated. But when sexual immorality is gratified, it leads to deeper and darker levels of bondage. When place is given to the spirit of lust, it not only drives the passions of our flesh but also engages us in a battle for *control*. None of us is invulnerable to the power of our sexuality becoming an instrument by which we are controlled.

THE BATTLE FOR CONTROL

A monitor in Pete's soul registered an internal witness at the first violation. But once he surrendered to the spirit of lust, Pete lost control. It is a great spiritual truth that *we become like the spirit to which we submit.* When we are submitted to the Holy Spirit, holiness is manifest in our lives. When we are submitted to the spirit of lust, as Pete found out, lust takes control of our lives (see 1 Pet. 1:13-16).

After Pete watched the movie, he felt justified in giving himself *license* to proceed. The Word of God speaks clearly against being *licentious*, referring to licentiousness as lasciviousness and wantonness in the *King James Version* and as lewdness in the *New King James Version* (see Mark 7:22; Rom. 13:13; 2 Cor. 12:21; Eph. 4:19). God's Word speaks so strongly because licentiousness bypasses God's monitors on the human heart that help to establish our values. The Christian is warned time and again against the licentious spirit that tries to justify immoral behavior. And, given license, the spirit of lust begins its deceptive seduction.

> We become like the spirit
> to which we submit.

Pete fell for one of the oldest lies in the book: masturbation is harmless. To the contrary, masturbation involves fantasy, which is related to idolatry; fantasy, pornography and masturbation are closely tied. Again, we are talking about an *image* behind which a demon spirit resides—whether that image be on paper, on screen or in a person's head. This is why I have never met a sincere believer who, committed to a full readiness to be honest about his or her deepest heart feelings, would not agree that he or she *knew* masturbation was wrong.

Masturbation opposes all that God intends for our self-giving (rather than self-centered) sexual capacity and fulfillment. It opposes self-discipline—that aspect of character and obedience so vital to being a disciple of the Lord Jesus Christ. Surrendering to the spirit of lust ultimately brings a person into a dimension of bondage from which it is difficult to be freed outside of the power of the Lord Jesus Christ. Efforts at overcoming through rededication seem futile apart from a power encounter with Jesus, involving confession, renunciation and deliverance.

The Word of God declares that the lust of the flesh and the lust of the eyes are not of God but of the world (see 1 John 2:16). The world's system encourages surrender to fantasy and pleasure seeking, and it glorifies the spirit of hedonism and avarice. People who surrender to that deception are letting their minds be shaped by the dictates of the world, which glamorize and validate moral corruption. We needn't even look as far as pornography to find that. Just step outside and take a glance at the billboards that use sexually explicit images to sell everything under the sun. Pornography pervades all facets of our culture, from ordinary TV programming to product packaging. These things all seek to engage the mind, provoke the flesh and pollute the soul.

I have counseled people from all strata of society—marrieds, singles, teens; the redeemed and the rebellious; the struggling victorious and the devastated fallen. No doubt it is because I am a man that I have felt particularly called by the Lord to speak to men. Yet what happened to Pete isn't the only way in which sex sin breeds an appetite for further immoral behavior; women who dabble in sexual flirtation or use sex as a means to obtain emotional or material favors from men find themselves equally surrendered to the spirit of lust, in bondage and struggling for control.

We are controlled by the spirit we submit to—being submitted to the Holy Spirit of Jesus Christ brings victory and sustains a joy-filled life of purity.

THE TORMENT OF SIN

Where do wars and fights come from among you? Do they
not come from your desires for pleasure that war in your members?
You lust and do not have.

JAMES 4:1-2

Pete and other believers like him who have given place to sexual sin are not happy people. The "wars and fights" referred to in this passage of Scripture are often in one's soul. Moral corruption and sexual sin drain the heart and mind of peace. When believers are walking in sexual impurity, there's a constant battle for control going on in their lives, as well as constant torment resulting from a parade of thoughts that they desperately wish would stop.

Let's consider a man who opened the door to sexual sin and found that it led to the ultimate in human depravity and transgression. His story captured the news headlines more than 20 years ago. I'm speaking of Ted Bundy, a good-looking fellow whose charming manner concealed a secret life as a manipulating sociopath, serial rapist and murderer.

In his last interview, conducted the day before his execution, Bundy amazingly described to Dr. James Dobson how he had grown up in a "solid, Christian home." Yet, Bundy admitted, his exposure at the age of 12 to pornography was the beginning of his descent into becoming a notorious serial killer. With sexualized violence fueling his fantasies, Bundy said that the moral inhibitions bred in him by his Christian upbringing were utterly overwhelmed by his addiction to pornography. He described a war raging inside of him between the right and wrong he'd learned as a child and his unbridled passion, driven by hardcore, violent pornography. When Bundy finally reached the edge, the last vestiges of restraint instilled in him as a Christian child were not enough to hold him back. He confessed to having sexually assaulted and killed more than 20 women, and he was executed in Florida in 1989 for the murder of a 12-year-old girl. His story illustrates the torment that can result from sexual impurity, and it provides frightening evidence of the capacity any person has for evil once the idol of pornography displaces the rule of Christ in the heart.[1]

LOVING DEVOTION TO CHRIST

What the Scripture calls us to is not the negation of our sexual capacities but *devotion to Jesus Christ*. Our love for Him will dictate obedience to the disciplines of His Lordship in our lives and will progressively bring the maximum release of everything we can be, including everything we can be sexually. That requires our coming under His Lordship—refusing to follow the pathway dictated by the world around us. In Pete's case, it would have taken the exercise of wisdom and the strength of good character to get up from the couch and leave his friends to watch the video without him. Better yet, Pete might have taken a stand by letting his buddies know he wasn't going to indulge in anything so demeaning. He might have been mocked for not wanting to be a "regular guy," but he also would likely have emboldened others to acknowledge the cheapness of such crudity.

Most of us, as believers, are faced with choices like Pete's on a regular basis, in the everyday world around us—whether it's lingering on the adult station while channel surfing or compromising our purity in reading material and other kinds of entertainment, often rationalizing this as necessary to stay current with the culture. But it takes character, conviction and conscience to go in the other direction, to separate ourselves from the crowd. Jesus gives us the reason for standing our ground, even when it means doing so alone: "Enter by the narrow gate; for wide is the gate and broad is the way that leads to destruction, and there are many who go in by it. Because narrow is the gate and difficult is the way which leads to life, and there are few who find it" (Matt. 7:13-14).

As we have already seen in a starkly literal sense, when it comes to sexual sin, we are confronted with a choice between life and death. Not only are our bodies at risk, but the spiritual and emotional damage can also be monumental.

KINGDOM DISCIPLESHIP AND ADVANCE

During my years of pastoral leadership in the men's ministry of my congregation, I came to realize that my target wasn't simply to confront masculine temptations, including sexual indulgence, but also to target the high goals and rich destiny of becoming the men God made us to be. I sought to cultivate in each man the desire to become a person through whom the kingdom of God would travel wherever he went—that Jesus would be seen in them and that each would be a light in the darkness of his world of influence.

Our lives as believers are not only about personal salvation and blessing, they are also about growth and discipleship. Discipleship involves *discipline,* the faithful exercise of which would have prevented the destructive turn of events in Pete's life. Discipleship is about believers' *advancing the kingdom of God on Earth* and becoming an answer to their own prayers—the prayer Jesus instructed His disciples to pray: "Your kingdom come. Your will be done on earth as it is in heaven" (Matt. 6:10).

Hereby, ministering agents of His kingdom are established, believers in Jesus Christ who live as "kings and priests"—faithful warriors and holy worshipers (see Rev. 1:6).

There's nothing that brings believers a more ready sense of disqualification than the condemnation, confusion and bondage that come from violating our covenant with God through sex sins. An adventure of curiosity sets the stage for us to be stricken with the paralysis of full-fledged bondage, as it did for Pete. Yet there is no one who is willing to turn from sin and repent whose life cannot be recovered and restored to wholeness, purpose and fulfillment in Jesus Christ.

HELP UNTO HOPE AND HEALING

"Let everyone who names the name of Christ depart from iniquity." . . .
In a great house there are not only vessels of gold and silver, but also of wood and clay, some for honor and some for dishonor. Therefore if anyone cleanses himself from the latter, he will be a vessel for honor, sanctified and useful for the Master, prepared for every good work. Flee also youthful lusts; but pursue righteousness, faith, love, peace with those who call on the Lord out of a pure heart.
2 TIMOTHY 2:19-22

Examining Myself

What sin have I allowed to snag me with its hook of bondage? Have I honored my covenant with God regarding the things I look at? Am I even just the slightest bit guilty of having used my sexuality to try to gain favor or recognition? What do I spend the most time thinking about—that is, "worshiping"? How honest am I willing to be with my own heart's convictions in the light of God's Word and the Holy Spirit's dealings?

Turning to the Lord in Prayer

*Father God, I come before You in humbleness and repentance
for having allowed myself to indulge in unworthy things, which
has created bondage in my soul. In the mighty name of
Jesus Christ, I renounce my participation in that sin and
declare that I will do it no more. I plead the blood of Jesus
Christ over my life, asking You to cleanse me from all
unrighteousness. Lead me in a plain path, Father God. Deliver
me from the evil one. Establish Your hedge around me; guard
my heart. I declare Jesus to be Lord of my life; and I surrender
my spirit, soul and flesh to Your will, Father God. Thank You
for redeeming me; I commit my ways to You from this day
forward. In Jesus' name I pray, amen.*

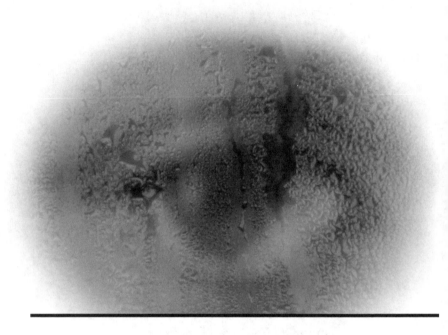

CHAPTER TEN

SEX SINS BREACH TRUST WITH THE WHOLE BODY OF CHRIST

For none of us lives to himself, and no one dies to himself.
ROMANS 14:7

The ninth reason why sex sins are worse than others is because sex sins breach trust with the whole Body of Christ. The impact of sexual impurity extends beyond our private lives and personal relationships to affect our brothers and sisters in the Lord.

Here is a case study of that in a letter that was written to me.

Dear Pastor Jack,

I've been a youth leader for two years. The kids—and their parents—relied on me to challenge and motivate them to meet high goals and standards, so they could grow up as rock-solid believers in an "anything goes" world.

Yet while I was encouraging the teens in my group to pledge abstinence until marriage, I indulged in a sexual liaison with a woman—an unbeliever. Somehow I convinced myself that because she wasn't a Christian, at least I wouldn't be compromising her testimony—that it was okay to have sex with her. I know it sounds ridiculous, but it's the truth—how blinding sin can be! Anyway, I never intended for it to be a long-term affair, but after several encounters, she became pregnant.

Suddenly, everything I had told those kids—dozens of teens who looked to me for spiritual leadership—now all seemed like baloney to them. The discovery of my hypocrisy resulted in an earthquake of impact—destructive to the kids, to their parents, to the church. And the byproduct was that many of them began to wonder about how real God really is—or isn't. Their reasoning was, Why should they believe what they'd been taught (including about walking in purity before the Lord), when a leader like me defiled the rules himself? They've been pushed into asking if the Jesus I had led them to praise is truly worthy—since His platformed advocates can live as unworthily as I did.

Chuck

The devastating results of Chuck's self-destructive indulgence and sin illustrate the influence, or impact, of a fallen church leader on the *whole* Body of Christ. It is admittedly a travesty that so many souls have had their faith shaken to the core because of sexual impurity on the part of spiritual leadership. Situations like Chuck's are nothing less than heinous and clear-cut works of our common adversary who knows that by striking the shepherd, the sheep will be scattered (see Matt. 26:31).

> ## Even the most obscure member has the potential to weaken the structure of Christ's Body.

However, let us not overlook how drastically *any* believer's sex sins make devastating inroads into the health of the Church. Whether or not sexual impurity or other failure becomes known publicly, the corrosive effect of even the most private sex sins needs to be clear in our perspective: Even the most obscure member has the potential—irrespective of his or her public influence or persona—to weaken the structure of Christ's Body. Like a single cancer cell loosed into the systems of a human body, any one of us can loose the death syndrome of sin into and through the Church. None of us lives or dies to ourselves!

When the apostle Paul wrote to the church at Corinth, "Your body is the temple of the Holy Spirit" (1 Cor. 6:19), he was writing about their physical bodies, but he was also writing to a *body of believers*. As well as addressing each man's and each woman's individual, personal body, the Bible also speaks to the *corporate* Body of Christ. God's Word is both explicit and emphatic when declaring the depth of our relationship to one another as brothers and sisters in Christ and the harm that the sin of even one member imposes upon the rest of the Body.

Just as the organs, nerves, bones and muscles of our physical bodies are dependent on one another for good health, so are we, as believers in Jesus Christ, interconnected and dependent on each other for our spiritual wholeness.

> For by one Spirit we were all baptized into one body. . . .
> For in fact the body is not one member but many. If one
> member suffers, all the members suffer with it; or if one
> member is honored, all the members rejoice with it. Now
> you are the body of Christ, and members individually
> (1 Cor. 12:13-14,26-27).

KINGDOM RULES

The self-indulgence that characterizes our society flaunts the ideal that people ought to be able to do what they want, when they want, with whomever they want. That theme is memorialized in the media with regard to the world's distorted idea of sexual liberation. Yet it's important for us as believers to be clear about the fact that the principle of Kingdom life—the one that calls us to accountability to one another by refusing to violate the Body of Christ with sexual sin—has no bearing on anyone who is outside of Christ. There is no righteous standard to which to call the world's people because the spirit of the world is blind and dead. Blind people cannot see the standards of the Kingdom, nor can dead people live up to them.

That does not mean that unbelievers do not suffer the horrendously destructive emotional, psychological, physical and spiritual consequences of sexual sin. Rather, it means that they are without the hope of recovery in those areas because they are lost in the darkness without Jesus, who is the light of the world: "He who follows Me shall not walk in darkness, but have the light of life" (John 8:12).

So let it be settled in our souls: When we, who have welcomed the living God into our lives, act in *any* manner that violates His kingdom order and ways, a horrible disruption occurs in the invisible realm. That disorder cannot be contained apart from confession, repentance and renunciation of sin. Otherwise, its effects will ripple through the Body of Christ, causing ever-expanding circles of corruption.

Neither you nor I have the right to live with anything less than a serious regard for this Kingdom principle: We do not have personal rights—we belong to one another. We are called to steward the trust we have in relationships with all our brothers and sisters in Christ; we are *one* with them in His Body.

THE RIGHT DECISION

Chuck left his church after he stepped down from leadership. Unfortunately, he stepped down too late—in reality he had *stepped down* before he *fell down*; that is, he had removed himself spiritually from responsibility, allowing satanic deception to have its place by reason of his submission to his own carnal desires. But along with stepping down, he might have more actively repented and sought forgiveness and restoration from his church rather than running away. In the wake of failures like Chuck's, responsive and responsible repentance turns the tide of evil before it sweeps outward. Repentance *reverses* what otherwise becomes a caustic spread of anger and distrust, often compounding sin as others choose to mirror the failure of the fallen, giving themselves license because of the sad example presented to them. How many have taken that route of carnal frustration, angrily muttering, "If that's all this is about, I'm outta' here!"

Thus we're called to uphold integrity's standards; but as that call echoes in our ears, again let me draw your attention to God's grace and goodness, dear one. Don't let a cloud of condemnation engulf you. Don't let dismay or discouragement provoke you to close this book, feeling your own failure or being angry as you wrestle with the memory of the failure of someone you trusted. Further, always keep in view the need to differentiate between people who experience an instance of stumbling and falling, and those who persist in sexual sin and argue some point of relative righteousness in continuing their lust-driven ways.

Victory is always within reach of those of us who call out to Jesus. Jesus is the deliverer—the forgiving Savior; and as His disciples, you and I are both immediate candidates for His mercy to overflow our failure if we come without defense and bow in abject humility. Praise God, our salvation is not contingent upon our sexual perfection. If we fail, forgiveness and restoration are possible. Then, renewing our commitment as disciples of Jesus Christ (answering His call to repentance and setting forth again to live within the disciplines fundamental to His living His life through us), we will find ourselves being lifted by His mighty hand to a place of restored purity and recovered vitality.

Sex sins breach trust with Christ's Body, to be sure. Yet, although it's true that forgiveness and full restoration are possible when a believer sincerely repents, *there's more!* If you're penitent, hear this truth: The same grace that covers your failure is also adequate to set in motion the removal of whatever poisoning impact your failure may have released.

Jesus is a wonderful, wonderful redeemer!

HELP UNTO HOPE AND HEALING

Every sin that a man does is outside the body, but he who commits
sexual immorality sins against his own body.
1 CORINTHIANS 6:18

Examining Myself

Where in my life have I breached trust with the Body of Christ by doing my own thing with regard to sex? Has anyone in my church fellowship ever broken trust with me by engaging in sexual sin? When they repented, did I respond to them with forgiveness or with cynicism?

Turning to the Lord in Prayer

Father God, forgive me for having violated my relationship
with my brothers and sisters in Christ and with You. I stand
accountable for those sins and deceptions that I tried to believe
were only about me. I welcome the light of Your truth to burn
out all deceit from my life. I repent and turn away from those
things which are not only unworthy of me but which also
wound and disable the Body of Christ. I ask You, in Your
great mercy, to release any who have responded with either
cynicism or unforgiveness—trapped in that bondage
by reason of what my sin ignited in them. Free them, dear
Lord, to restore our fellowship again. Thank You for Your
restoration, Lord. Today I take my rightful place as
Your disciple. In Jesus' blessed name, amen.

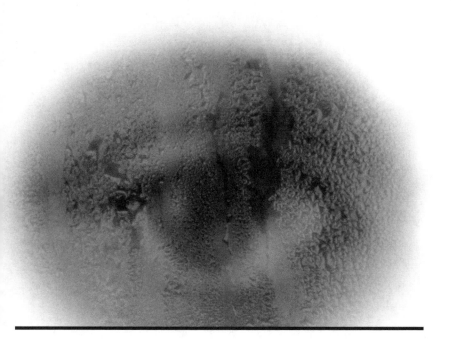

SEX SINS ASSAULT THE PURE LORDSHIP OF JESUS CHRIST

*Do you not know that your bodies are members of Christ? Shall I then
take the members of Christ and make them members of a harlot?
Certainly not! Or do you not know that he who is joined to a harlot is
one body with her? For "the two," He says, "shall become one flesh."
But he who is joined to the Lord is one spirit with Him.*

1 CORINTHIANS 6:15-17

Finally, and most profoundly, sex sins are worse than other sins,
not only because they cripple our own lives and wound
others,

not only because they compromise our ability to enter
    into and maintain healthy relationships,
not only because they open up the possibility of suffer-
    ing that extends far beyond ourselves,

but because sex sins assault the pure lordship of Jesus Christ.

This assault on the lordship of Jesus Christ is a fact we can hardly bring ourselves to look at because it is so shockingly improper and yet so tragically true. Although the writer of the following letter didn't realize it, the perplexing perspective her believing father offered cuts to the heart of why sex sins are, indeed, worse than others.

Dear Pastor Jack,

When I was a kid growing up, I always thought it was weird that when I left our house, my dad would say to me, "Take Jesus with you." It didn't matter where I went or what I was going out to do. I could be just going to the store or to school—he'd say the same thing every single time. Whether I went to the mall or the movies, my dad would always tell me, "Take Jesus with you."

By the time I was out of high school, I was pretty wild and rebellious. I was into a lot of things I knew my parents disapproved of—things that were really bad. And I can remember thinking that my dad must have been off his rocker saying to me, "Take Jesus with you," when he knew I was heading out the door to go meet some guy to have sex.

Rhonda

We began this book by recognizing that it is the *damage* that sex sins cause in the lives of those who have been redeemed by Jesus Christ that makes them worse than other sins; it is not because there is any order of sin that is more or less sinful. *All* sin separates us from God; *all* sin wounds the Body of Christ; *all* sin grieves the Holy Spirit. But sexual sin, unlike other sins, has a way of establishing deeper bondage in the life of a believer, hindering at a greater dimension his or her availability to be a vessel of the Holy Spirit's ministry to others, and initiating devastating consequences for generations to come. We've examined the personal damage that sex sins cause in the life of the believer who indulges in them, and we've also looked at the collateral damage they cause in a believer's relationships with others.

We are *all* sinners saved by grace (see Eph. 2:5); and while sex sins are not harder for God to forgive, we who are disciples of Jesus Christ are called to be *more* than forgiven—we are called to be *holy* (see 1 Pet. 1:15). As disciples, our conduct ought to reflect the moral and ethical holiness—the *wholeness*—of God's character. Nowhere is the requirement of that discipline more profound than in looking at how sex sins assault the pure lordship of Jesus Christ in the life of a believer.

THE SINLESS NATURE OF JESUS CHRIST

For we do not have a High Priest who cannot sympathize with our weaknesses, but was in all points tempted as we are, yet without sin.
HEBREWS 4:15

The Word of God says that *Jesus was without sin,* that God "made *Him who knew no sin* to be sin for us, that we might become the righteousness of God in Him" (2 Cor. 5:21, emphasis added). It may seem needless in a book written primarily to believers in Jesus Christ to underscore the sinless nature of our Savior, because without His sinlessness, Jesus' sacrifice on the cross would not have fulfilled Scripture nor redeemed our lives. And yet the spirit of the world pursues every avenue it can to diminish Jesus—who lived, loved and ministered as a single adult—to its level.

> It is the *damage* that sex sins cause in the lives of those who have been redeemed by Jesus Christ that makes them worse than other sins.

While the purity of Jesus Christ is fully established in the Word of God, that doesn't mean that there was anything less than human about Him. Hebrews 4:15 says that He was "in all points tempted as we are." Yet, unlike us, Jesus was born of a virgin and walked in absolute, sinless perfection. That means He kept His mind, and most certainly His relationships, pure and without moral compromise.

Much speculation has been made about Jesus' relationships with women, in particular with Mary Magdalene. The constant proposition, made even on occasions by preachers, is that Mary Magdalene was Jesus' romantic heartthrob. We've all heard it proposed that she was a young, attractive, former prostitute who had everything from an infatuation to a sexual relationship with Him. Yet there is *nothing* in the Bible that says Mary Magdalene either was young or a prostitute, let alone that anything impure ever transpired between her and the Savior. In fact, it is possible that Mary Magdalene was an older woman, a peer of Jesus' mother, Mary.

Of course it's reasonable to suppose that women were attracted to Jesus, but that wouldn't have been because there was anything seductive or alluring about Him. It was because there was something so *wholesome* in Jesus that women knew He was a man whom they could *trust*. In the culture of that era, when women had so few resources of their own and were so vulnerable to exploitation, they recognized the purity of Jesus and could tell that approaching the goodness they saw in Him was *safe*. Without fear of being manipulated or abused, women knew they could come to the Lord and find genuine answers to the deepest needs of their souls.

THE REAL TEMPTATION OF CHRIST

Therefore, in all things He had to be made like His brethren, that He might be a merciful and faithful High Priest in things pertaining to God, to make propitiation for the sins of the people. For in that He Himself has suffered, being tempted, He is able to aid those who are tempted.
HEBREWS 2:17-18

The spirit of the world has a vested interest in disqualifying the pure lordship of Jesus Christ by turning Him into a man who surrendered to temptation. The currently fashionable secularization of Christ—infiltrating books, films and intellectual discourse—falls in line with other attempts to strain the spiritual truth out of the gospel and turn it into philosophy or humanism.

In 1988, the film *The Last Temptation of Christ* ignited

controversy by suggesting not only that Jesus and Mary Magdalene may have had a romantic relationship between them but also that Jesus might have elected not to die on the cross. The movie's defenders claimed it was only an allegory, yet the implant of *doubt* in people's minds regarding the character and nature of the Lord is one avenue of deceitful strategy by the adversary.

More recently, it was proposed in the pseudohistorical book *The Da Vinci Code*, as well as in a preposterous "investigative" report by a major television network titled "Jesus, Mary and Da Vinci," that Jesus married and also fathered a child.[1] That any member of the Christian community would bother to take these ideas seriously is astonishing, because they dismiss the central fact of Jesus' identity and purpose in the world: The sinless Son of God, sacrificed on our behalf to redeem us from our sins.

By making Jesus a fallen human being like the rest of us, Satan has neutralized Jesus as the Savior. In deceiving people to believe that sin (or sinlessness) doesn't make any difference to who Jesus was, the prince of this world successfully disarms humankind's perceived need for repentance and salvation, giving the world all the justification it needs to pursue its self-initiated, perverted decline to nowhere. It's a perfect plan by the enemy of our souls to swindle people into thinking that their lives don't need to be redeemed by Jesus Christ. In this setting, God's magnificent plan of salvation becomes nothing more than a superstitious, or anecdotal, folktale.

The Bible says that the suffering and temptation Christ endured were on our behalf, and out of that, He is able to help us resist temptation in our lives (see Heb. 2:17-18). Temptation in the life of Christ was overcome for our sakes, not indulged in for His own.

JESUS WITH US WHEREVER WE GO

The Bible says that when a believer engages in sexual sin, he or she is taking a member of Jesus Christ and joining it to sexual immorality. When Rhonda's father told her, "Take Jesus with you"—fully aware that she was headed to a motel to engage in illicit sex—*he knew exactly what he was saying.* This is a brutally graphic image, but it must be engraved upon our minds for the full impact of what this book is saying to the believer: In the final analysis, sex sins are worse than other sins because in sexual immorality, *a believer prostitutes the body of Jesus Christ.*

Scripture confronts those of us who have been redeemed by Christ, whose bodies are now members of Christ: "Shall I then take the members of Christ and make them members of a harlot? Certainly not! Or do you not know that he who is joined to a harlot is *one body* with her? For 'the two', He says, 'shall become one flesh'" (1 Cor. 6:15-16, emphasis added). The unmistakable and painfully grotesque extension of the truth we have just looked at in the previous chapter—that sex sins breach trust with the whole Body of Christ—is that whatever act of indulgence of sexual sin we engage in with our bodies, we are also obliging the Spirit of the Lord Jesus Christ, who dwells in us, to commit that act along with us.

Who among us can imagine ourselves pressing the Lord Jesus to have sex with another person? Who would dream of forcing Him upon the bed and driving Him into sexual intercourse? Or making Him stand in front of a toilet and masturbate? Yet that is exactly what is being done when the indwelling Christ is forced into submission to our human wills.

As we have already established, the Lord lives in us, and our bodies are not our own; therefore, whatever we do with our bodies *Jesus does with us.* This must be riveted in our minds as believers: Wherever we go, whatever we do, we *are* taking Jesus Christ with us. When my hand steals, it is Jesus stealing. When my tongue lies, it is the tongue of Jesus lying. And when I engage in sexual immorality, it is Jesus whose body and lordship in my life I am degrading. He who died to redeem us from sin has called us to live in obedience to His will, not our own. We who have received the life of the living God in ourselves are compelled by the Holy Spirit, who now dwells in us, to walk in purity before Him.

A SLAP IN THE FACE

When Anna's and my children were small, there were a few, infrequent occasions when I seemed unable to communicate to them how deeply concerned I was about something they were doing. We sought to correct our children more than once, but the message just didn't seem to register. As their father, I felt hurt by this, and though it wasn't a matter of their being rebellious, I sensed I wasn't being clear enough for them to get the message.

The few times that I felt it necessary to do what I'm about to share with you, I would be in tears as I called the child involved in to see me. I would make certain we had eye contact and would say, "Dad is really upset about this, and you don't seem to be catching on. You are just sitting there; you hardly seem sensitized to what I've said to you. Reach here to me." I would take that child's forearm, with his or her hand free, and instruct, "Open your hand and make it stiff." And then, as hard as I could, I would take my child's arm and slap my own face with his or her hand. *It would hurt us both!* And it would leave a stinging, red mark on my face and make my child's own hand smart. My child would look at me in shock and then would begin to whimper "Daddy!" and would start to cry. How much my child had hurt me would finally register in his or her soul. My children weren't only wounding themselves by their behavior; they were hurting their father as well.

We are admonished by Scripture not to grieve the Holy Spirit because it is by the Holy Spirit now dwelling in us that we have been "sealed for the day of redemption" (Eph. 4:30)—an act of grace possible only because of the sacrifice of our sinless Savior, Jesus Christ. We who name the name of Jesus are accountable to embrace the character and nature of God, in whose image we were created, and to preserve the pure lordship of Jesus Christ in ourselves by walking in purity and holiness in our thoughts, words and deeds. For us to pursue a lifestyle that is anything less than that is as wounding to Father God as slapping Him in the face.

And yet, even still, just as I embraced my repentant children—once the shock of what they had been doing to themselves and to me registered in their souls, and it was clear that they would no longer pursue that wrong path—so also through the sacrifice of His own precious Son, Jesus, Father God extends His arms of love, forgiveness and restoration to those of us who sincerely, humbly, truthfully and transparently enter into confession, repentance and renunciation of our sins.

HELP UNTO HOPE AND HEALING

Contend earnestly for the faith which was once for all delivered to the saints. For certain men have crept in unnoticed, who long ago were marked out for this condemnation, ungodly men, who turn the grace of our God into lewdness and deny the only Lord God and our Lord Jesus Christ.

JUDE 1:3-4

Examining Myself

In what ways have my actions grieved the Holy Spirit, hurt Father God and denied the pure lordship of Christ in my life? Is there any place to which I am ashamed to have taken Jesus with me?

Turning to the Lord in Prayer

Lord, forgive me for having violated the purity of Your life in mine through sexual sin. Teach me to contend earnestly for the faith despite the world's call to indulge my flesh. I renounce every worldly spirit I have given place to and declare I will no longer allow the enemy of my soul to deceive me into a lifestyle that is less than the one that You have designed for me. Restore Your lordship in my life, as I surrender and submit all that I am to You. In Jesus' name, I pray, amen.

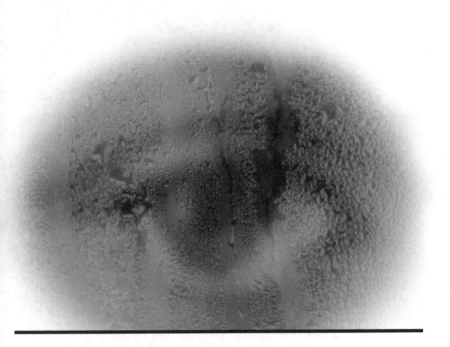

CHAPTER TWELVE

THERE'S HOPE FOR TOMORROW

For You have delivered my soul from death, my eyes
from tears, and my feet from falling.
PSALM 116:8

Together, we have examined how the snares set by the adversary as a result of sexual sin or violation can become embedded in one's soul, and how that damage stains, subverts, pollutes and disables a believer's identity, emotionality, creativity, confidence and authority. Even if a person is not actively engaging in sexual sin, the wound to his or her soul from a past violation can be like the hole left behind by a nail that has been driven into a place it doesn't belong and then yanked out by the claw of a hammer. Childhood abuse, exposure to pornography and youthful sexual experimentation all create bondage that is often reinforced by an adult believer's subsequent compulsive and desensitized forays into sexual sin.

I've written this book to equip believers with the tools of biblical wisdom, real-life understanding and practical application necessary to receive or to minister wholeness, health, restoration and recovery from the damage caused by sexual sin. Along our journey together, we've had the opportunity to examine ourselves; to turn away from any habit of or indulgence in sexual sin that we may have willingly (or unknowingly) given place to in our lives; and to invite the Holy Spirit to purge, cleanse, heal and restore us to wholeness. The prayers for help unto hope and healing at the end of every chapter incorporate many of the elements of deliverance ministry. If you are a believer in Jesus Christ and you have not yet invited the Lord to fill you with His Holy Spirit, I truly hope that you will desire the overflow of God's grace, love, power and gifts in your life. To receive that promised fullness, we have placed a prayer you may pray in appendix 2. Also, a prayer for renouncing sex sin and inviting deliverance has been placed in appendix 3.

To gain still greater perspective on the truths we have studied together in this book calls for a more complete examination of the processes of release from the residue of sex sin. I have pointed out the pathway to God's forgiveness, which His abundant grace affords us beyond our failures. But it is very often the case that the deep emotional impact and the psychological and personal scarring left in the wake of sexual violation require further healing ministry.

That's the reason a list of suggested resources has been prepared to help the reader address the matter of sexual integrity (see appendix 5). No single book—short of a massive, intimidating volume—can cover the broad aspects of this vital subject so essential to our well-being and fulfillment and to our joy and obedience in serving Christ.

FORGIVEN, FREED, ENABLED AND EMPOWERED

Allow me to conclude with the following words of basic assurance and grounding, pointing to the path of hope for your future walk in the blessings of sexual integrity and purity of life.

We began this study by looking at the biblical story of the woman caught in the act of adultery. Jesus stood between her and the death sentence of her accusers, bringing her to peace and freedom in Him. While God never condones sin, the Savior who stands between us and an eternal death penalty offers forgiveness, deliverance and restoration to those of us who will repent from our sins and turn to Him. This is God's desire for *all* humankind, for He "did not send His Son into the world to condemn the world, but that the world through Him might be saved" (John 3:17).

In the light of that great sacrifice made by Father God on our behalf, there is no more appropriate way to conclude our examination of why sex sins are worse than other sins than with the words—and *in the power*—of our Lord and Savior, Jesus Christ: "*Go and sin no more*" (John 8:11, emphasis added).

They are words of more than forgiveness; they are filled with His power and promise. He is not only saying, "Don't do that anymore," but your Lord and mine is also saying,

Go! And as surely as I've forgiven you, I'm going beside you. As surely as My blood has washed you, My Spirit will empower you. As absolutely as I have broken the power of sin, I will establish My victory over it in your life, in your mind and in the members of your body. Commit all that to Me—life, mind and body—and I tell you: You will sin no more!

So hear Him, dear one. And *go!*

A Prayer for Receiving Christ as Lord and Savior

It seems possible that some earnest inquirer may have read this book and somehow still never have received Jesus Christ as personal Savior. If that's true of you—that you have never personally welcomed the Lord Jesus into your heart to be your Savior and to lead you in the matters of your life—I would like to encourage you and help you to do that.

There is no need to delay, for an honest heart can approach the loving Father God at any time. So I'd like to invite you to come with me, and let's pray to Him right now.

If it's possible there where you are, bow your head, or even kneel if you can. In either case, let me pray a simple prayer first and then I've added words for you to pray yourself.

My Prayer

Father God, I have the privilege of joining with this child of Yours who is reading this book right now. I want to thank You for the openness of heart being shown toward You and I want to praise You for Your promise, that when we call to You, You will answer.

I know that genuine sincerity is present in this heart, which is ready to speak this prayer, and so we come to You in the name and through the Cross of Your Son, the Lord Jesus. Thank you for hearing.[1]

And now, speak your prayer.

YOUR PRAYER

Dear God, I am doing this because I believe in Your love for me, and I want to ask You to come to me as I come to You. Please help me now.

First, I thank You for sending Your Son, Jesus, to Earth to live and to die for me on the cross. I thank you for the gift of forgiveness of sin that You offer me now, and I pray for that forgiveness.

Forgive me and cleanse my life in Your sight, through the blood of Jesus Christ. I am sorry for anything and everything I have ever done that is unworthy in Your sight. Please take away all guilt and shame, as I accept the fact that Jesus died to pay for all my sins and through Him, I am now given forgiveness on this earth and eternal life in heaven.

I ask You, Lord Jesus, please come into my life now. Because You rose from the dead, I know You're alive and I want You to live with me—now and forever.

I am turning my life over to You and from my way to Yours. I invite Your Holy Spirit to fill me and lead me forward in a life that will please the heavenly Father.

Thank You for hearing me. From this day forward, I commit myself to Jesus Christ, the Son of God. In His name, amen.[2]

A Prayer for Inviting the Lord to Fill You with the Holy Spirit

Dear Lord Jesus,

> *I thank You and praise You for Your great love and faithfulness to me.*
>
> *My heart is filled with joy whenever I think of the great gift of salvation You have so freely given to me,*
>
> *And I humbly glorify You, Lord Jesus, for You have forgiven me all my sins and brought me to the Father.*
>
> *Now I come in obedience to Your call.*
>
> *I want to receive the fullness of the Holy Spirit.*
>
> *I do not come because I am worthy myself, but because You have invited me to come.*
>
> *Because You have washed me from my sins, I thank You that You have made the vessel of my life a worthy one to be filled with the Holy Spirit of God.*
>
> *I want to be overflowed with Your life, Your love and Your power, Lord Jesus.*
>
> *I want to show forth Your grace, Your words, Your goodness and Your gifts to everyone I can.*
>
> *And so with simple, childlike faith, I ask You, Lord, fill me with the Holy Spirit. I open all of myself to You to receive all of Yourself in me.*

I love You, Lord, and I lift my voice in praise to You.
I welcome Your might and Your miracles to be manifested in me for
Your glory and unto Your praise.

I'm not asking you to say "amen" at the end of this prayer, because after inviting Jesus to fill you, it is good to begin to praise Him in faith. Praise and worship Jesus, simply allowing the Holy Spirit to help you do so. He will manifest Himself in a Christ-glorifying way, and you can ask Him to enrich this moment by causing you to know the presence and power of the Lord Jesus. Don't hesitate to expect the same things in your experience as occurred to people in the Bible. The spirit of praise is an appropriate way to express that expectation; and to make Jesus your focus, worship as you praise. Glorify Him and leave the rest to the Holy Spirit.

A Prayer for Renouncing Sex Sin and Inviting Deliverance

Prayer

Heavenly Father, I come to you in the name of Jesus. I come with repentance and humility to receive the cleansing I need. I believe the blood of Jesus cleanses me from all sin. Holy God, I desire cleansing and freedom from all sexual sin and impurity and all unholy soul ties.* I confess and repent of my own sexual sins and of the sexual sins of my former generations.**

I specifically confess as sin and I repent of giving place to sexual lust: lust of the eyes, lust of the flesh, impure thoughts and all sexual fantasies.

I repent for all involvement with any kind of pornography. I specifically repent of the viewing or use of pornographic photos, books or magazines, pornographic movies, computer pornography and Internet chat rooms.

*I repent of all involvement in the sins of fornication, adultery,
infidelity and prostitution. I repent of all involvement in perverted sex, including homosexuality, sodomy, sadism, orgies,
group sex and sexual activity with animals.*

*Heavenly Father, I specifically repent of all attitudes and all
words or actions forcing or requiring my spouse to participate
or take part in any sexual acts which to them are degrading
and distasteful or which violate their conscience before God.*

*I repent of sexual self-gratification and self-indulgence, includ-
ing masturbation, exhibitionism and Internet or telephone
sex. I also repent of all attitudes, actions and spirits associated
with sexual pride, sexual power, sexual conquest, entice-
ment and seduction.*

*And now, Father God, I renounce*** all these sexual sins: all
sexual immorality, fornication and adultery, lust of the flesh,
perversion, pornography, sexual abuse, selfishness and manipulation. I renounce all unclean spirits behind these sins. I
renounce all unholy soul ties. I want nothing more to do with
them or with any sexual sin, in the name of Jesus.*

*In the name of Jesus, through the power of the Holy Spirit, I
break the yoke of bondage from all sexual sins. I choose from
this moment on to walk sexually pure before my God.*[1]

DEFINITIONS

*Soul Ties

A mental or emotional attachment of the soul to a person or object, involving both the mind and emotions, resulting in the influencing of the choices of our will.

There are *good soul ties* (see Gen. 2:24, 44:30, Deut. 10:20, 1 Sam. 18:1 and 2 Sam. 20:2) and *destructive soul ties* (see Gen. 34:1-3, Num. 25:1-3, Josh. 23:12-13 and 1 Cor. 6:16).

**Generational Ties

Keeping mercy for thousands, forgiving iniquity and transgression and sin, by no means clearing the guilty, visiting the iniquity of the fathers upon the children and the children's children to the third and the fourth generation.

EXODUS 34:7

Although the sins of former generations are not credited to our account, there is still something very destructive that takes place. If the sins of our parents are unrepented of, the spiritual influence behind those sins tends to press in on us the next generation (i.e., children of abusive parents are more likely to succumb to abusive behavior in their own life).

***Renouncing

The night is far spent, the day is at hand. Therefore let us cast off the works of darkness, and let us put on the armor of light.

ROMANS 13:12

And have no fellowship with the unfruitful works of
darkness, but rather expose them.
Ephesians 5:11

An action taken by the believer in Jesus Christ against the forces of darkness that declares all previous association to be cancelled. All words, agreements or actions that opened the door to demonic influence are now broken.

COLORADO STATEMENT ON BIBLICAL SEXUAL MORALITY

God intends sex to be a source of satisfaction, honor, and delight to those who enjoy it within the parameters of the moral standards He has established. Biblically speaking, human sexuality is both a *gift* and a *responsibility*. At creation, the gift of sex was among those things God declared to be "very good" (Gen. 1:31). What's more, the sexual relationship is invested with a profound significance in that it brings together a man and a woman within the context of the shared image of God (Gen. 1:27). Because sex is God's idea, and because it touches the image of God in human life, it is very important that the holiness of sexual behavior be diligently preserved. In fact, sexual behavior is moral only when it is holy (Eph. 1:4; 5:3; 1 Thess. 4:3-7; 1 Pet. 1:14-16).

Not only is sex good in itself; it is also given to serve good purposes. At creation God made it very clear that sex functions in two ways: it generates "fruit" (Gen. 1:28); and it enables relational "union" (Gen. 2:24). In other words, sexuality does not exist merely for its own sake. Rather, sex fosters human nurturing, both through the union of husband and wife and also through the enrichment of society through the building of families and communities. God also made sex to reflect the mysterious spiritual relationship He will one day enjoy with all redeemed humanity following the wedding supper of the Lamb (Rev. 19:7,9).

According to God's plan, sexual intimacy is the exclusive prerogative of husband and wife within the context of marriage. Sexual morality, on the other hand, is everyone's concern. It matters to single individuals, to families, and to society. Most of all, it matters to God.

Sex that honors God's guidelines and standards is pleasurable. He designed sexual activity to be physically enjoyable, emotionally satisfying, psychologically fulfilling, and spiritually meaningful because He delights in the joys and pleasures of His creatures (Song of Sol. 4:1-16). Men and women who honor God's standards for sexual behavior please Him as well as themselves (1 Cor. 6:20; also note analogy in Isa. 62:5).

But while sex is designed to be pleasing, not all sexual pleasure is ethical. Feelings are extremely unreliable as guides to the morality of sex. As a matter of fact, it is possible for sinful men and women to experience a form of physical enjoyment and degrees of emotional, psychological, and spiritual fulfillment even in sexual conduct that God considers abhorrent. For this reason, the Bible gives many solemn warnings against appealing to human passion or lust as the basis for our definition of moral sex (Rom. 1:24,26; 13:13-14; 1 Thess. 4:5; 2 Tim. 2:22; 2 Pet. 3:3; 1 John 2:15-17; Jude 18). Our sex lives are moral only when conducted according to God's standards. When engaged in according to these guidelines, sexual activity is enriching, fulfilling, and eminently blessed.

We want to warn against deceptions that hinder or forestall this blessing of God upon our enjoyment of the wonderful gift of sex. We also want to help men and women understand God's good plan for sexual conduct, and thereby to realize all the joy, satisfaction, and honor God offers to sexual creatures made in His image.

Based on our understanding of biblical teaching, we make the following declarations. We do not claim that these declarations cover everything the Bible says on sexual morality. But we do believe they highlight standards that are critical for our time.

1. **Desire and experience cannot be trusted as guidelines to the morality of sex** (Rom. 8:5-8; 13:14; 1 Cor. 2:14; 1 Thess. 4:3-5; 2 Tim. 2:22; James 1:14; 1 John 2:15-16; Jude 19). **Instead, the morality of sex is defined by God's holiness** (Lev. 20:7-21,26; 1 Cor. 6:18-19; Eph. 1:4; 5:3; 1 Thess. 4:3-7; Heb. 13:4; 1 Pet. 1:15-16).

Thus we affirm that men and women are free to enjoy sex in any way that honors God's holiness. We affirm that God made sex to be physically enjoyable, emotionally satisfying, psychologically fulfilling, and spiritually meaningful, and that only sex that honors God's holiness can fully realize the complexity of His design at every level. We affirm that concepts of sexual morality founded upon anything other than God's holiness always pervert God's standards of sexual moral purity.

2. **God's standard is moral purity in every thought about sex, as well as in every act of sex.** Sexual purity can be violated even in thoughts that never proceed to outward acts (Job 31:1; Matt. 5:28; Phil. 4:8; James 1:14-15). Sex must never be used to oppress, wrong or take advantage of anyone (1 Thess. 4:6). Rape, incest, sexual abuse, pedophilia, voyeurism, prostitution and pornography always exploit and corrupt and must be condemned (Lev. 18:7-10; 19:29; 2 Sam. 13:1-22; Prov. 6:26; 23:27; Matt. 5:28; 1 Thess. 4:3-7; 1 Pet. 4:3; 2 Pet. 2:13-14).

Thus we affirm that God requires sexual moral purity in thought as well as in deed. We affirm that sexual desire must be disciplined to be moral. We affirm that thoughts of indulging sexual desire by outward acts of sexual sin are inward sins of lust.

We deny that stimulating lust by images of sexual sin can be moral at any age or under any circumstances. We believe that no sexual act can be moral if driven by desires that run contrary to the best interests of another human being. We believe no sexual act can be moral that treats persons as impersonal objects of sexual lust. We reject the idea that thoughts about engaging in sexual sin are not immoral if not expressed in outward acts. We reject the idea that pedophilia, voyeurism, prostitution or pornography can ever be justified.

3. God's standards for sexual moral purity are meant to protect human happiness (Prov. 5:18-19; 6:32-33; John 15:10-11), but sex is not an entitlement, nor is it needed for personal wholeness or emotional maturity.

Thus we affirm that unmarried singles who abstain from sex can be whole, mature persons, as pleasing to God as persons who are faithful in marriage. We affirm that sexual celibacy is a worthy state for mature men and women (Matt. 19:12; 1 Cor. 7:1,8; Rev. 14:4), and that lifelong celibacy can be a gift from God (1 Cor. 7:7). We affirm that freedom for service without obligations to spouse and children is a worthy advantage of the unmarried life (1 Cor. 7:32-35). We reject the idea that persons are not "whole" without sexual intercourse. We affirm that all persons, even unmarried teenagers, can rely on God for strength to resist sexual temptation (1 Cor. 10:13). We deny that unmarried teenagers must have sex and cannot abstain from sex before marriage.

4. God calls some to a life of marriage, others to lifelong celibacy, but His calling to either state is a divine gift worthy of honor and respect (1 Cor. 7:36-38). No one is morally compromised by following God's call to either state, and no one can justify opposing a divine call to either state by denying the moral goodness of that state.

Thus we affirm that God is pleased with those He calls to serve Him through the loving expression of sexual intimacy in marriage. We also affirm God is pleased with those He calls to special witness and service through a life of celibacy apart from marriage. We reject the idea that God's Word ever represents the loving expression of sexual intimacy in marriage as morally compromised.

5. **Sexual behavior is moral only within the institution of heterosexual, monogamous marriage.** Marriage is secure only when established by an unconditional, covenantal commitment to lifelong fidelity (Gen. 2:24; Mal. 2:14-15; Matt. 19:4-6; Mark 10:6-8; 1 Cor. 7:39; Rom. 7:2; Eph. 5:31), and we should not separate what God has joined (Mal. 2:14-15; Matt. 19:6; Mark 10:9). Christians continue to debate whether there are a limited number of situations in which divorce is justifiable (Deut. 24:1-4; Matt. 19:9; 1 Cor. 7:15), but all agree that divorce is never God's ideal; lifelong commitment should always be the Christian's goal.

Thus we affirm that God established the moral definition of marriage, and that it should not be changed according to the dictates of culture, tradition, or personal preference. We deny that the morality of marriage is a matter of mere custom, or that it should be allowed to shift with the tide of cultural opinion or social practice. Furthermore, we affirm that God views marriage as an unconditional, covenantal relationship that joins sexual partners for life. We oppose the reduction of the moral obligations of marriage to a business contract. We do not believe that divorce for reasons of dissatisfaction, difficulty, or disappointment is morally justified.

6. **Marriage protects the transcendent significance of personal sexual intimacy.** Heterosexual union in marriage expresses the same sort of holy, exclusive, permanent, complex, selfless and complementary intimacy that will someday characterize the union of Christ with the redeemed and glorified Church (Eph. 5:28-33; 1 Cor. 6:12-20).

Thus we affirm that intimate sexual union in marriage is a reflection of the intimate moral and spiritual union Christ will someday enjoy with the redeemed and glorified Church. We do not agree that the meaning and purpose of human sexuality can be defined on the basis of personal preference or opinion. We oppose the idea that sexual morality is simply a matter of culture, tradition, or individual aspiration.

7. **Sex in marriage should be an act of love and grace that transcends the petty sins of human selfishness,** and should be set aside only when both partners agree to do so, and then only for a limited time of concentrated prayer (1 Cor. 7:3-5).

Thus we affirm that sex in marriage should be enjoyed without selfishness. We do not believe that sex should be withheld as a way of controlling, punishing, or manipulating the behavior of a spouse. We reject the morality of any sexual act, even in marriage, that does not express love seasoned by grace. We believe no sexual act can be moral if it is driven by selfishness or ambition for power.

8. **Sex outside of marriage is never moral** (Exod. 20:14; Lev. 18:7-17,20; Deut. 5:18; Matt. 19:9,18; Mark 10:19; Luke 18:20; Rom. 13:9; 1 Cor. 6:13,18; Gal. 5:19; Eph. 5:3; 1 Thess. 4:3; Heb. 13:4). This includes all forms of intimate sexual stimulation (such as foreplay and oral sex) that stir up sexual passion between unmarried partners (Matt. 5:27-28; 2 Tim. 2:22). Such

behavior offends God (Rom. 1:24; 1 Thess. 4:8) and often causes physical and emotional pain and loss in this life (Prov. 5:3-14). Refusal to repent of sexual sin may indicate that a person has never entered into a saving relationship with Jesus Christ (Rom. 1:32; 1 Cor. 6:9-10; Eph. 5:3-5; Jude 13; Rev. 22:15).

Thus we affirm that God's blessing rests on sexual intimacy only when it occurs within the boundaries of marriage. We deny that sex outside of marriage is justified for any reason. We reject the idea that sexual intimacy outside of marriage can be moral if partners are honest, consenting, or sufficiently committed. We oppose the portrayal of sexual sin as a way of enhancing the popular appeal of entertainment. We reject the idea that sex between unmarried teenagers is acceptable if it is "safe." And we do not believe that churches should welcome into fellowship any person who willfully refuses to turn away from the sin of living in a sexual relationship outside of marriage.

9. **The Old and New Testaments uniformly condemn sexual contact between persons of the same sex** (Lev. 18:22; 20:13; Rom. 1:26-27; 1 Cor. 6:9; 1 Tim. 1:10); and God has decreed that no one can ever excuse homosexual behavior by blaming his or her Creator (Gen. 2:24; Rom. 1:24-25).

Thus we affirm that moral sex is always heterosexual in nature. We affirm that God gives strength to His people when they ask Him for help in resisting immoral sexual desires, including desires for homosexual sex. We affirm that God has perfect knowledge concerning human sexual biology and made no mistake in prohibiting homosexual sex without qualification or exception. We deny the claim that science can justify the morality of homosexual behavior. We reject the idea that homosexual attraction is a gift from God (James 1:13). We deny the idea that homosexual relationships are as valid as heterosexual relationships. We do not agree with those who claim that it is sinful to make moral judgments that favor heterosexual behavior over homosexual behavior.

10. **The moral corruption of sexual sin can be fully forgiven through repentance and faith in Christ's atoning work** (1 Cor. 6:9-11; 1 John 1:9), but physical and psychological scars caused by sexual sin cannot always be erased in this life.

Thus we affirm that God fully forgives all who repent of sexual sin. We believe that relationships broken by sexual sin can be restored through genuine repentance and faith. We deny that there is any sort of sexual sin God cannot forgive. We oppose the idea that victims of sexual infidelity or abuse should never forgive those who have sinned against them.

11. **Christians must grieve with and help those who suffer hardship caused by sexual immorality, even when it is caused by their own acts of sin** (Rom. 12:15; Luke 19:10). But we must give aid in ways that do not deny moral responsibility for sexual behavior (John 8:11).

Thus we affirm that God calls Christians to love all who suffer social isolation, poverty, illness, or the burdens of unplanned pregnancy and single parenting, whether or not it was caused by their own sexual sin. We believe Christ set an example of loving ministry to those who suffer from the results of their own acts of sin. We reject the idea that our obligation to alleviate human suffering is valid only if such help is "deserved."[1]

Suggested Resources

Books by Jack Hayford from Regal Books
Available at www.regalbooks.com

The Anatomy of Seduction: Defending Your Heart for God
> Protect your spiritual integrity through this biblical guide that provides real-world solutions for avoiding seduction of the mind and body.

Blessing Your Children
> Transmit a spiritual inheritance of substance and worth to the next generation by learning how to bless your children.

I'll Hold You in Heaven
> Read the classic best-seller that offers healing and hope for the parent who has lost a child through miscarriage, stillbirth, abortion or early infant death.

Living the Spirit-Formed Life
> Rediscover the power and blessings of such basic disciplines as prayer and fasting, daily worship and the release of repentance and forgiveness.

OTHER RESOURCES BY JACK HAYFORD

Available at www.jackhayford.org
or by calling toll-free (800) 776-8180

The Beauty of Spiritual Language: Unveiling the Mystery of Speaking in Tongues (Book)
> Learn how speaking in tongues is neither gibberish nor emotional exuberance but is an intimate encounter with the heart of God.

Cleansed for the Master's Use (Audiocassette or VHS video)
> Find a pathway of sanctification and deliverance in these three powerful teachings.

The Encyclopedia of Deliverance: Finding Freedom Through Christ and His Cross (24-audiocassette album)
> Explore in depth an array of specific topics on spiritual warfare and liberation from bondage.

The Finger of God (Booklet)
> Use this concise study to understand the demanding ministry of deliverance that leads God's people from spiritual bondage to divinely intended freedom.

Rebuilding the Real You: God's Pathway to Personal Restoration (Book)
> Study the book of Nehemiah, which unfolds a clear picture of the nature and work of the Holy Spirit to assist the believer in rebuilding life's broken places.

Also on DVD: *Nehemiah: Pictures of the Holy Spirit*

INTERNET RESOURCES FOR EDUCATION AND SUPPORT

- Jack Hayford Ministries (www.jackhayford.org)
- The King's College and Seminary (www.kingsseminary.edu)
- Cleansing Stream Ministries (www.cleansingstream.org)
- Focus on the Family (www.family.org)

ENDNOTES

Preface

1. "Facts About HIV/AIDS—Global" *WHO/UNAIDS*. http://www.unaids.org/wac/2002/facts-global.pdf (accessed January 2, 2004).

Chapter 2

1. The people you will meet in this book are representative of the many who have written or come to me seeking counsel in dealing with issues of sexual sin. Some of their stories and letters have been edited into composites; and all names have been changed so as not to violate anyone's privacy, confidence or trust.

Chapter 7

1. James Vicini, "Top Court Rejects Baby Death Conviction Appeal," *Washingtonpost.com,* October 6, 2003. http://www.washingtonpost.com/ac2/wp-dyn/A51315-2003Oct6?language=printer (accessed January 2, 2004).
2. Abby Goodnough, "Florida Executes Killer of an Abortion Provider," *New York Times*, September 4, 2003, National Report, p. A12.
3. "Facts About HIV/AIDS—Global" *WHO/UNAIDS*. http://www.unaids.org/wac/2002/facts-global.pdf (accessed January 2, 2004).

Chapter 8

1. Joint United Nations Programme on HIV/AIDS, quoted in "Basic Statistics," *CDC,* December 3, 2003. http://www.cdc.gov/hiv/stats.htm (accessed January 1, 2004).
2. "The Fight Against AIDS and Tuberculosis," *Bill and Melinda Gates Foundation,* 2004. http://www.gatesfoundation.org/GlobalHealth/HIVAIDSTB/ (accessed January 1, 2004).
3. "Basic Statistics," *CDC,* December 3, 2003. http://www.cdc.gov/hiv/stats.htm (accessed January 1, 2004).
4. Charlene Laino, "AIDS: Worst Yet to Come—U.N.:70 million may die of HIV over next 20 years," *MSNBC,* July 2, 2003. http://www.msnbc.com/news/774926.asp (accessed August 25, 2003).
5. Charlene Laino, "AIDS Creates Global Orphan Crisis—25 million kids

predicted to lose a parent by 2010," *MSNBC,* July 10, 2003. http://www.msnbc.com/news/777815.asp (accessed August 25, 2003).

6. John Richens, John Imrie and Helen Weiss, "Sex and Death: Why Does HIV Continue to Spread When So Many People Know About the Risks?" *Abstinence Clearinghouse,* November 25, 2003. http://abstinence.net/ library/index.php?entryid=648 (accessed January 1, 2004).

7. Marc Lacey, "For Ugandan Girls, Delaying Sex Has Economic Cost," *The New York Times,* August 18, 2003, section A, p. 4. http://www. nytimes.com/2003/08/18/international/africa (accessed August 25, 2003).

Chapter 9

1. Ted Bundy, interview by James Dobson, transcript, Focus on the Family, 1989. http://www.family.org/resources/itempg.cfm?itemid=932 (accessed January 2, 2004).

Chapter 11

1. "Jesus, Mary and Da Vinci: Exploring Controversial Theories About Religious Figures and the Holy Grail," *ABC News,* November 3, 2003. http://abcnews.go.com/sections/World/Primetime/davinci031103.html (accessed March 26, 2004).

Appendix 1

1. Jack Hayford, *I'll Hold You in Heaven* (Ventura, CA: Regal Books, 2003), pp. 38-39. Used by permission.

2. Ibid., pp.39-40.

Appendix 3

1. With thanks to Pastor Chris Hayward, President, Cleansing Stream Ministries. Used by permission.

Appendix 4

1. "Colorado Statement on Biblical Sexual Morality," copyright © 2003, Focus on the Family. All rights reserved. International copyright secured. Used by permission.

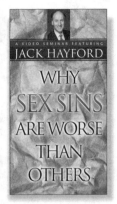

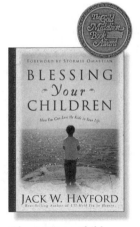
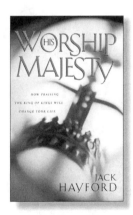

Take Hold of the Victory!

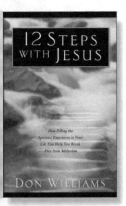
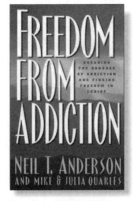

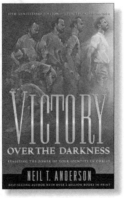
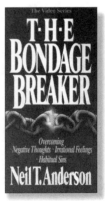